The Kingdom Within

By Yvonne Prentice

Copyright

Dedication

I dedicate this book to my children.

My desire is that you will enjoy reading about our friend Holy Spirit and that you will each pass on what you have received to the next generation.

Acknowledgements

First and foremost eternal thanks to my God and very closest companion, Holy Spirit. It has been at Holy Spirit's prompting that this work has been written, and I pray it is pleasing to God.

I thank my family: Mum and Dad who gave me so much.

My dear husband: Bob, who is my biggest fan and encourager.

My children: Ben, Kyle, Rachel, Abby and Caleb - who have taught me so much, given love and constructive feedback, who listen to my ideas, and encourage me.

To the following dear people, without whose help this work would never have been completed, I say thank you so much:

To Rachelle Lavergne-Dixon: who edited this work thank you for labour of love, enthusiasm, creativity, wisdom and support which has given this project life. You are such a blessing

My daughter Rachel: my proofreader and computer wonder, who has countless times saved me hours of frustration. You have more than repaid me for the times of reading your many university papers. Love you, dear.

Many thanks to Karen Trory: for her proofreading and advice.

Many thanks to those who have blessed me with their creative gifts, which can be admired in the beautiful cover of this book:

My daughter, Abigail Cook: artist of "Kingdom Release" which has so beautifully illustrated Holy Spirit's flow released from each of us. Thank you to Tricia Tumibay, for the cover layout and her enthusiasm.

To Reverend Virginia Tilstra: who has been a wonderful friend and has encouraged me to write and told me she "trusts the Holy Spirit in me".

Contents

Suggestions for Using This Book

In order for this book to be of most benefit to you, I have included questions that you may take into your times with Holy Spirit.

For many people, much deeper revelation into a particular spiritual truth is received when they dedicate time to listening to God through stillness or soaking prayer[1]. For example, I had noted the verse on the Sevenfold Spirit of God as I read my Bible, and knew that I needed to understand this concept, so I took time over the course of a week to be still, listen, and meditate upon it. Each day I dedicated time to one of the aspects of the Sevenfold Spirit and used listening prayer or soaking to hear God's voice with all of my senses. I then wrote what He had shown me and asked further questions using two-way journaling to hear God through His voice or spontaneous thoughts[2]. Chapter 2 of this book was borne out of what God showed me in that time, and thus provides an example of what can result from meditation and listening prayer.

You may wish to use this material as a group by reading each section, practicing listening prayer and meditating, and then sharing together the revelation of truth that Holy Spirit has unveiled to you.

I pray you will not only enjoy reading this book and pondering its topics, but that you will use it as a launching pad for hearing and experiencing Holy Spirit more and more. May you connect with God in a deeper way as you grow in your knowledge and love of Him.

---

1   See "Listening Prayer", Chapter 6.
2   See "Hearing", Chapter 5.

Introduction – Connection to God

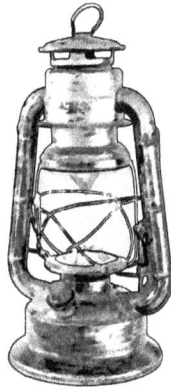

The Apostle Paul wrote in Galatians 3:26-4:7: You are all sons of God through faith in Christ Jesus, for all of you who were baptized into Christ have clothed yourselves with Christ. There is neither Jew nor Greek, slave nor free, male nor female, for you are all one in Christ Jesus. If you belong to Christ then you are Abraham's seed, and heirs according to the promise. What I am saying is that as long as the heir is a child, he is no different from a slave, although he owns the whole estate. He is subject to guardians and trustees until the time set by his father. So also, when we were children, we were in slavery under the basic principles of the world. But when the time had fully come, God sent His Son, born of a woman, born under law, to redeem those under law that we might receive of His Son into our hearts, the Spirit who calls out "Abba, Father." So you are no longer a slave, but a son; and since you are a son, God has made you also an heir.

This scripture is talking about the change God made in the religious community of the day, Judaism, when His son Jesus Christ gave His life to enable all people everywhere to become sons of God. This transaction: Jesus' death for our life, is sealed by the Holy Spirit who comes to connect us with God. He can do that because He is God, and having all power He comes to empower us to live from our true spiritual nature.

I found this amazing truth - that I am now a son of God

- to be exciting. Unfortunately it was not actualized for the first twenty years of my Christian experience. This disconnect between what God intends for His people and what we experience is, I have realized, a common issue among Christians. I found this is due to several factors, which I will attempt to address in this work on Holy Spirit.

My initial misunderstanding of how to please God – that is, by learning more and more about Him and trying to be good - seemed to be upheld by the teaching I received which emphasized striving and straining to work at the Christian life, sanctification growing out of human effort. As I am not much of a disciplined person by nature, it was just a matter of time before failure and disillusionment hit me full force.

In response to this I became more determined in my attempts to behave as a good Christian woman should, which was perpetually followed by disappointment. This destructive cycle only proved to reinforce low self-worth and embarrassment about my falling short, which in turn led to blockages in my friendships with God and other people. Another negative effect of this self-defeating pattern was that I felt the need to hide the real (far-from-perfect!) me from those in my Christian community.

Grace for life in God: Although most of us agree that God is gracious, merciful, and kind, we often do not live in accordance with that knowledge. We practice life through the misconception that we are to live by rules of religion and regulations of Old Testament law. Many Christians thus believe that self-effort is the way to achieve a lifestyle that will please God, yet human discipline and resources are not adequate to achieve what God designed to do through the power of His Holy Spirit working in us.

If, on the other hand, we choose to live in the truth of God's grace, we are able to be open with God about our inabilities and allow Him to do good work from within us. Holy Spirit has been given to us not only to convict us of our inability to love and obey God but to conform and empower us to live as Jesus did.

Jesus Christ modeled the perfect life of love and power as He lived among mankind. We can follow His example if we live in the realization that we are unconditionally loved by our Father God, that He has given us His grace (unmerited favour and empowerment) to live as His children, and that He has provided everything we will need to live out of our new nature.

Many believers are held back from living in love and power as Jesus did, due to the misconception that, "If God wants me to be healed, to see visions, to hear His voice, or do any supernatural act, He will do it. I am willing to receive but He will have to initiate." This thinking may cause passivity that risks severely limiting how fully we live out of our divine nature[3].

Let us rather be inspired by Jesus' ministry here on earth, entering into active agreement with God as we learn to listen and see like Christ; He did not stand idly waiting for a sovereign act of God when performing His many miracles! Jesus Christ implemented His Father's kingdom and gave expression to the divine power with which His Father directed Him to use.

In writing the following pages, I do not want to merely inform you about the Holy Spirit, nor is it my wish to attempt a complete study on His work or to fully describe His inward ministry; my desire is that you would receive enough insight to stir you into encountering Him and experiencing a life of union with God. I hope you will come into a deeper agreement with Holy Spirit's unction and direction.

You will find at the end of each topic suggested meditation or journaling exercises. These are to help direct you to the Holy Spirit for His personal input as you digest each aspect being presented. I pray that as you read and ponder you will be helped by the disciplines and practices I have described. As you learn to hear and listen to God's sweet voice I trust you will grow deeper in your love and knowledge

---

3   Of course, the sovereign intervention of God moving upon a person spontaneously can and does happen without limiting us. In fact it is by God's initiation that we come to Him for the gift of salvation and the Holy Spirit's indwelling presence.

of Him.

Chapter 1 – My Journey, Coming to Know Holy Spirit

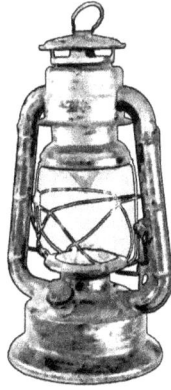

At the age of six I began to have a strong desire to go to church. I lived in Sydney, Australia at the time and a young neighbour, who was a new Christian, offered to take me to the little Methodist Church on the hill close to our home.

The Sunday school had a loving and peaceful atmosphere, and I felt God's presence. I became fascinated with Jesus, who was depicted as a gentle shepherd and loving father in white robes. Although it wasn't until many years later that I really got to know this wonderful Saviour, I began to long to be close to God.

As an adult I actually thought that somehow God and I were a long way apart and didn't realize that in those very early childhood experiences God had been softly speaking. He began to show Himself to me in dreams and in my imagination, through daydreaming or, as I would now call it, meditations.

God gave me wonderful dreams that created a deep awareness that He is real and cares for me but He also gave me many warning dreams which, because of my unreceptiveness, came to pass as a teenager. I didn't understand that He was trying to warn me and save me from hurt and disillusionment.

It wasn't until my twenties, when I was married and had our first child, that the longing to know God became so intense I could not ignore it anymore. Through extremely difficult circumstances, my searching for answers and my openness to His call brought me to the discovery of what it meant for Jesus to love me. I accepted the truth of His sacrifice for my restoration to the Father and was born again into the family of God.

Yet as the years went by, theology based upon what I read and was taught caused me to think pleasing God meant pushing myself to try to become a good person. I began to work really hard at that: my desperate efforts to be a good wife and mother, to serve others, and to stop sinning certainly kept me busy, as well as feeling stressed and inadequate!

Fortunately, God is determined to orchestrate events and to touch our spirits so as to show us that we are dry and thirsty for Him. That is just what Jesus did in me. My heart continued to be stirred and I longed for a real experiential friendship with God. Some of my Christian friends tried to assure me that I had found the answers I needed, that salvation was all that mattered and any other experience was not godly, but my spirit yearned for something deeper, and I could not ignore that conviction.

In fact, I felt that if what I was experiencing as a Christian was all there was - the human effort and self-discipline – I had enough. I needed to have more than just the mental knowledge of God, I desired to experience Him. I craved a touch, a taste, to hear a word; I had to have something that came unmistakably from God... or I would give it all up and quit!

I see now that my frustration over the first two decades of my Christian experience arose from the Holy Spirit remaining much of a mystery to me. I did not understand that at conversion, when I invited God to take over my life, He did do just that and sent Holy Spirit to fuse with my human spirit, permanently. Holy Spirit is the power source of the kingdom of God - He is the gift of God and the source of every enabling, that we may be conformed to the likeness of Jesus Christ! Despite all of this good news, I was not deeply aware of the role of Holy Spirit in my spiritual life. So many years of wandering, impatience, and frustration had me at a breaking point[4].

It was in the midst of these very feelings of isolation and confusion, through a crisis of belief, that Holy Spirit was drawing me to Himself. Indeed, the Lord had set me up so I would truly encounter Him at just the right time. He must have been rubbing His hands together when I was at my wits' end because at last He had my attention! I was ready to stop the crazy merry-go-round ride of self-effort, to be quiet enough to hear and still enough to receive His embrace.

I experienced the significant shift I needed at a retreat where I was introduced to the fact that I needed to formally renounce past practices and beliefs which were ungodly. Even though I had long since realized the error and no longer practiced them, the lack of repentance in those areas had resulted in a dull emptiness, which had blocked me from hearing God properly. Once I had repented and received God's cleansing my desire to hear from God Himself quickened and I was filled with Holy Spirit.

God had been so wonderfully present the entire time, waiting patiently for me to stop trying so hard. I would love to take back the time I spent busying and tiring myself, but He was teaching me many lessons and now that I can receive His thoughts I see God doesn't waste even our mistakes. He has radically changed my life as I spend time in His presence, listening and communing.

It has been more than fifteen years since my renewal encounter. I have been moving up God's learning curve as He has taught me to be attentive to His voice in its diverse forms and enter into His rest. Part of the learning process for me has been the wonderful privilege of creating personal prayer blankets; it is largely through this ministry that I have learned about the symbolism through which the Holy Spirit chooses to speak. I am still so excited when He gives me a

---

4   Perhaps such times can help us understand what the Israelites endured during those long forty years in the desert! I am thankful my dry time was for a mere twenty years. I have noted that most Christians do experience a period of wandering in the desert of striving or religion at some point in their walk of faith - it seems to be a process many must go through.

little mystery to decode, a dream or vision to interpret, or He speaks through some other way in the wonderful language He fashions uniquely for each person. All of this shows how intimately He knows us and cares for us - how deeply he desires to engage in communion with us.

As I review my life, God has been there all along, gently nudging me, quietly calling, despite the fear and noise that seemed overwhelming at times. Finding the way home to my heavenly Daddy took many turns that included some lessons learned the hard way, but it did lead to peace and abundant life with God – Father, Jesus, and Holy Spirit – being my closest companion.

My journey of knowing Holy Spirit is certainly not complete and so this writing by no means is a comprehensive manual on all one can know about Him. It is my pleasure nonetheless to share some pointers that I have found a help to knowing and flowing with the wonderful Spirit of God.

Suggested Meditation or Journaling Exercise
Lord Jesus, please speak to me about the journey You have taken me on in discovering You. How would You have me continue?

Progressing Toward Union with God
We see in Genesis 1:2 that the Spirit brooded over the dark formless void. Have you ever wondered what the verb in that well-known verse means? Here is a definition of "brood":

    a) ponder

    b) sit on eggs to hatch them

    c) hover closely[5]

This brooding of the Holy Spirit was not only true at the inception of creation, but remains true of our individual spiritual inception: Holy Spirit broods over each of us, each

---

5   All definitions taken from: Barber, Katherine, ed. The Canadian Oxford Dictionary. Toronto: Oxford University Press, 1998.

person's soul being as a void until it is filled by Him, bringing us life.

The Genesis verse also states that God speaks, and light is birthed. Indeed, we see throughout the Bible that God is light: the Son Jesus is the light of the world, and the Holy Spirit gives light from God to us. It is God's brooding over the human soul and spirit that births in us enlightenment to God and His ways[6].

Obligation

In this atmosphere of being nurtured by the Spirit, we begin to awaken to God's existence. In my life this brooding began at six years of age. For many people this early stirring can be encouraged or thwarted by the adults around them. My heart was satisfied for a time just knowing God was kind, like the Sunday school depiction of the gentle shepherd, but as other interests captured my attention the early curiosity seemed to subside.

The later prompting of the Spirit came in the form of questions about eternity and conviction of sin. Even though the questions were unclear to my conscious mind, my spirit knew them and the Holy Spirit's brooding drew me to search for answers.

Eternal questions of life's meaning, destiny, and our human condition of lacking of connection to God – all of these stirred me. I have since come to recognize that the initial answers revealed were the unveiling of my obligation to God. I simply had to respond; I was compelled to, and gladly received the mercy and grace given so lovingly for me.

Indeed, the revelation of Jesus' payment on our behalf demands a response from each human being. In other words, to be awakened to the personal nature of God and the sacrifice of Christ's life on the cross requires an answer, as would a proposal to one's beloved.

The reality is that we need to connect with our Creator. The One Who designed us has good purpose in mind

---

6   See John 3:6, 3:19-21, and 8:12.

and is the author of the truth, and yet many people never awake to God. Although the Spirit broods over all of us, some remain disconnected and the basic step of faith remains unaccomplished.

Fortunately, many do acknowledge their obligation and gratefully enter into a life of connection to God: we receive peace with God and the gift of His precious Spirit as our seal of belonging[7]. Our spiritual nature is radically changed in that we are then partakers of the divine nature and have become sons of God (inheritors of the Kingdom of heaven).

As we enter into this journey with God we come to understand with greater clarity how our lives depend upon the provision of God in every aspect of life. Ultimately, we connect with our need of Him.

Need

As we begin our new life of communion with God, we will start to understand and sense the need of Christ in our lives not only for that initial connection but also because we can do nothing of value without Him. We notice that our own human motives and agenda are not in tune with God's. In our own strength, we cannot love unconditionally, and do not see or treat others with the grace and mercy that Jesus modeled. Humbly turned to Holy Spirit, we constantly realize our lack and our need of Him. The awareness of our condition, that we are in want, is ever increasing.

As we grow in our life in union with Holy Spirit, He teaches us to yield to His promptings. Gradually, more of our faculties become infused with Holy Spirit's graces, gifts and fruit. We understand our need for daily refreshing and empowering of God's presence; relying and perpetually drawing on the goodness of our Creator brings us into a life of flow.

This continuous cycle – our need perpetually satisfied by God's supply –is His design for life. It is symbolized around

---

7   See "Symbolic Descriptions", Chapter 2.

us through elements of nature, such as the water, oxygen, and nitrogen cycle on Earth. The planet is replenished by its author who has built in the need for, and provided the supply of the water, nitrogen, and oxygen that sustains life. Likewise, He has fashioned us to need His presence and to be fed in a continuous cycle from within by His essence, which is Holy Spirit. His Spirit is given to us for the purpose of perpetuating spiritual life as the cycles in nature do from sustained perpetual feeding on what the creator has given.

There is another even deeper revelation of connection with God than that of our need. This is the passion of God and the fulfillment of the human soul.

Desire

The dictionary defines the word "desire" as:

a) an unsatisfied longing or craving.

b) wishful wanting.

c) expression of request.

While this allows us to note the types of desire, we also recognize how distinct it is from obligation and need.

When it comes to my need for God, it is simply my human condition; even the lowest, most basic state of being alive and breathing require His touch, so I can safely assume all of us need Him whether we know it or not.

Change happens as we act on the deeper need to connect and agree with God. Scripture encourages us in Romans 12:1, Let your body be a living and holy sacrifice. When we think of what He has done for us, is this too much to ask? Although being motivated by the need for God is good, it is nonetheless the least we can do.

When we come to God because we desire to know Him, to enjoy the sweet presence of Holy Spirit and to be a friend of God, not only is the need understood but the heart has more devotion. The dichotomy of spiritual exchange between God and mankind is that longing and desire become stronger as we enter into this closeness. We grow in our love and desire as we connect with His great love and desire for us.

We become so enamoured by His presence and completely devoted to a life of intimacy with Him that nothing else will satisfy: the old, mediocre Christianity is ruined for us as we grow addicted to Him! This state is something that is to be experienced and enjoyed by each of us, for it is the fulfillment of spiritual life. God is the well-spring of life, goodness, peace and indeed every imaginable blessing.

As we approach Him from a place of desire we are no longer hindered by feelings of inadequacy which come from obligation; when we come desiring, we are not constrained by the thought of how well we are responding to His commands due to our need of His power. From the deeper level - a heart of desire for God, just to be with Him and drink in His love - we are liberated.

A wonderful example of the deepening of our relationship with God is that of the difference between a young couple raising their children and that of a mature married couple who have remained faithfully in love for many years after the children are raised. In the first example the young couple are really in a mutually dependant situation. They very much need one another to each do their part to parent and provide a loving home. Their love bond is very strongly based on their mutual need to rely on each other's support to complete the tasks at hand.

On the other hand, the mature couple are no longer in need of each other's support to raise the family now: their bond is that of mutual love and enjoyment of each other. They are together simply because they love and cherish their time together; they are content and satisfied simply living as one.

So it is as we mature in our love for God. Our need develops into the beautiful pleasure of fellowship with Him. Out of desire for Him comes freedom to fully enjoy the delights of knowing God. Father God, Jesus Christ, and Holy Spirit become to us our all in all. He feeds us the food and drink of His presence[8]. At the deepest level of our being we draw from Him and He enjoys our companionship also. God enjoys the fruit He has planted in our lives, the fruit of His love and presence.

As we develop or friendship with God and pure desire for Him grows we rise up into alignment with His heart. God has never been in the place of obligation toward us. Nor has He needed us, for He is self-sufficient and self- sustaining. God has been waiting for us in the place of desire. Since He first had kind thoughts of creating us His desire was for deep intimate friendship with us. Our growth into deep desire for communion with our maker is the satisfaction of His design; that at long last we may love with the same heart, though we will never reach the degree with which He loves, we can know His purity of motive to just simply be together.

This calling toward desire for God is ours as His children. The journey of delight and transformation into our union with God and living through this imparted divine nature is where we find rest for our souls. The Scriptures only once encourage us to strive, and that is to enter into His rest. We must enter, we need to enter, and ultimately we desire to enter into the presence of God where we find our rest.

Suggested Meditation or Journaling Exercise

God, where am I currently in my life with You?

Jesus please speak to me about living in deeper desire for You.

Lord, speak to me about spiritual hunger.

---

8   See Song of Songs 2:3-6.

Chapter 2 – Knowing Holy Spirit

Knowing about the Holy Spirit and actually knowing the person of Holy Spirit are very different positions to ponder. For twenty years of my Christian life I understood a bit about the Holy Spirit. My knowledge was quite limited but I would have said I grasped the main concepts: Holy Spirit is the third person of the Trinity; He is the Spirit of Christ which indwells every believer who confesses that Jesus Christ is Lord, repents of sins, and invites Him to take over their lives.

This basic knowledge satisfied my mind those many years as I busied myself with the many Christian activities and studies recommended to me. I built up a theology about God based upon what I read and was taught in church all of which kept me busy thinking and doing. This activity occupied my "God time" and, ironically, prevented me from spending the quality time with God that would have allowed me to get to know Him and experience the presence of Holy Spirit.

Did you notice the absence of the word "the" before I referred to Holy Spirit? I think it would be very odd if anyone called me "the Yvonne"! Even though I could be referred to as the Reverend Yvonne, I really do not want my friends or acquaintances to do that; it would be very awkward for me and I would assume the other person was keeping our relationship in very formal parameters.

Of course, I understand that God the Holy Spirit

deserves the honour and right of the formal title "the Holy Spirit", as do "the Father" and "the Christ, the Lord", such that in this book I will use that title at times. Nevertheless, Holy Spirit is my closest companion, my dearest friend, my teacher, my encourager, and even like a mother or father to me. I never called my mother by the formal title but used the endearment of Mum (Australian spelling) and the same for my father, he was always Dad. They would have been hurt had I addressed them with any less intimate names, and I think Holy Spirit feels like that about His dear ones.

After all, He is sharing the same house: our bodies - specifically our human spirits - are His home. We could not be more intimately related than that! So that is why I most often use the name Holy Spirit but you will occasionally find I use His title too, with "the".

While we are on the subject of how I refer to this wonderful friend of mine I would like to address the topic of the pronoun "him". I could use "her" equally, without fear of divine retribution, because Holy Spirit is genderless. Nonetheless, while spirit does not have a gender, the Bible refers to the Holy Spirit with the male gender most often, so I have chosen to do the same.

I have found Holy Spirit to be more loving than a mother and the most perfect benevolent father. Indeed, as we will see His names and attributes go far beyond the most perfect person no matter whether they are male or female! The nature and characteristics of Holy Spirit go far beyond human description, let alone the parameters of gender roles; with this in mind, I hope I will not offend my readers by most often using male pronouns for the sake of aligning with the bible.

Following is a brief description of the Spirit of God:

- **Holy**: morally excellent; to be revered, devoted to; consecrated and sacred.

- **Spirit**: the vital animating essence of a person or animal; the intelligent non-physical part of a person; a rational or intelligent being without a material body; supernatural being.

Holy Spirit is the Spirit of Jesus Christ. As such, He exemplifies all of the qualities of Jesus and discloses the nature of God to us, as well as imparting to us the divine nature of God; this gift of God's nature in us, granted through Holy Spirit, is our deposit or seal, the proof that we are children of God.

The name of the third person of our triune God describes His purity, His devotion to divine uniformity, and His set-apart nature. He is completely different from every other spirit, being one of a kind, uncreated, eternal, completely and perfectly unified in the Trinity.

Holy Spirit is our counsellor, comforter, teacher, revealer of truth, our healer, and our peace. He is personal, not a force or power but One Who has the ability to be grieved or pleased. He communicates with us and quickens us to the ways of God.

In simpler words Holy Spirit's personal nature encompasses His having emotions and wanting to communicate and participate with us in our day to day lives. He is a friend who loves and also really likes us. He has lots of wonderful plans, purposes, and ideas to share with us because He, along with Father and Jesus, created us to be the object of His great love.

Love needs to be given, and God's love needs a recipient, people who will take that love and enjoy it with all the benefits that God's amazing love brings. We are, you see, the offspring of the great loving king, the God of the universe, Who loves perfectly and Who desires that we know His love and receive His Kingdom.

His Names

Spirit of Christ, of Jesus, and of the Son
These titles show that Holy Spirit not only is the essence of Jesus Christ, He has come to exalt and glorify Jesus.

Comforter
Here we see that Holy Spirit is to carry on the work of Jesus in encouraging, counselling, and consoling God's people.

Spirit of Grace
There is a promise in the Old Testament that the Spirit of grace and supplication would be given. The New Testament describes those who wilfully sin as insulting the Spirit of grace referring to Holy Spirit.

Spirit of Life
He imparts life and gives us a new way to live through the law of the spirit of life described in Romans 8.

Spirit of Truth
He is truth who guides us into all truth.

We also see in Scripture the names;
Spirit of Adoption (Romans 8:15)

Spirit of Holiness (Romans 1:4)

Spirit of Prophecy (Revelation 19:10)

Power of the Highest (Luke 1:35)

Symbolic Descriptions

Breath or Wind
Pnuma, the Greek word for "breath" or "wind", is given to Holy Spirit in both the Old and New Testaments. See, for example, John 3:8.

Clothing
Holy Spirit is the clothing of power that Jesus said would endow or dress us from on High. He also clothes us with His fruit. See, for example, Luke 24:49.

Deposit
The down-payment of our divine nature, given in seed form at salvation, is sealed by our being filled with Holy Spirit. He establishes our legal position in the family of God as we grow closer to Him. See, for example, 2 Timothy 1:14.

Dove
The Spirit is described to hover and brood, as well as being seen at Jesus' baptism to descend upon Him in bodily form. See, for example, Mark 1:10.

Fire

Jesus said that the Holy Spirit would come to baptize with His own Spirit and with fire. In the book of Acts, we see Jesus' words fulfilled with the sign of tongues of fire appearing on the heads of the disciples. See, for example, Luke 3:16.

Flow of Living Water

This description gives insight into what it feels like for us to live from the unction of God. Jesus is the one who spoke the words, "If you are thirsty, come to Me! If you believe in Me, come and drink! For the Scriptures declare that rivers of living water will flow from the heart of those who believe in Me." (John 7:37-39) So we see that Holy Spirit flows like a river from within us. He is a river of life to us and imparts all of His nature and attributes to us as we yield our souls to His promptings.

As we attune to Him we experience the flow of Holy Spirit within our own spirit and soul. We will be addressing in this teaching how we can become accustomed to the flow of Holy Spirit within us and begin to release through us the river of life that is His very presence.

Oil

Jesus' name of Messiah means anointed one. Jesus made the statement in Luke 4:18 that He was anointed by the Spirit to preach good news. Also the anointing from The Holy One teaches us the difference between truth and falsehood[9].

Seal

We are, at conversion, sealed with the Holy Spirit as our guarantee of ownership, the symbol being that of belonging, protection, and responsibility taken by God on our behalf[10]. Holy Spirit is like the seal of God's approval.

Wine

Holy Spirit is likened to wine because we come "under the influence", similarly to those drinking alcoholic drink. Indeed, some of the manifestations of being filled with Holy Spirit can at times have the appearance of drunkenness. The early

---

9   See 1 John 2:27.
10   See Ephesians 1:13-14

disciples themselves were accused of being drunk when they were filled with the Spirit at Pentecost, as told in Acts 2:15!

We gather from this last symbol a connotation of joyfulness, playfulness, freedom, fun, and good cheer.

Sevenfold Spirit

Holy Spirit is the member of the Trinity Who joins us to God. When He makes our human spirit His resting place, we are connected to God in the most amazing, personal way. He makes it possible for us to turn inward to God by way of His divine nature. He imparts Himself with His very attributes now accessible to us through the Spirit to Spirit connection. In fact the apostle Paul prayed for the Ephesian church that they would have spiritual wisdom and understanding so that they might grow in the knowledge of God[11].

> And the Spirit of the LORD will rest on Him – the Spirit of wisdom and understanding, the Spirit of counsel and might, the Spirit of knowledge and the fear of the LORD. (Isaiah 11:2; see also Revelation 3:1 and 4:5.)

The Spirit Who Rests upon Us

Rest: to be still or asleep, to refresh oneself or recover strength; relieve or refresh.

At salvation the Spirit of Christ comes and makes His home within our spirit. First the Spirit of God cleanses and completely mingles with our spirit so that we become one with God in our spirit. This is the reason nothing can separate us from the love of God as mentioned in Romans 8:38 and John 14:16-17.

Holy Spirit comes as the representative of Jesus Christ to inwardly witness with our spirit that we are His. In John 14:26 we are told He comes to counsel and remind us of all that Jesus has taught. In verse 27 Jesus says He is leaving us a gift, peace of mind and heart, which comes by the inner presence of Holy Spirit.

The remaining attributes of the sevenfold Spirit of

---

11   See Ephesians 1:17.

God are mentioned in pairs. Wisdom and understanding, for instance, team together to bring us into inner agreement with the nature of God Himself.

Wisdom and Understanding
Wisdom: applying experience and knowledge together practically (wise: demonstrating knowledge, judgment, discernment and prudence).

Understanding: the ability to reason and comprehend to perceive and interpret a situation.

Proverbs 1:2-4 sets up the book of Proverbs as instruction that will make the simple-minded clever. What the wisdom in Proverbs has done for the natural mind, the Holy Spirit takes to a new level, giving inner wisdom and understanding to the spirit of man supernaturally, surpassing human resources. When we attune to the Spirit's inner unction, wisdom and understanding will flow, bubbling up to our minds from within, so that we are able to operate in comprehension of a situation and bring interpretation and practical discernment for appropriate action.

Counsel and Might
Counsel: to give advice; consultation; a plan of action.

Might: great bodily or mental strength, power to enforce one's will; the utmost of one's power.

The Spirit of counsel and might advises us of the strategies of heaven and graces us with strength to carry out heaven's plan. Holy Spirit speaks spirit to spirit with us to counsel us so that we are enabled to yield to His divine plans for us.

The Knowledge and Fear of the Lord
This is the foundation of true knowledge. To know God and honour Him by giving Him first place in our lives is essential to accessing and knowing Him.

As we get to know God we are awed by Who He is. His power, greatness, wisdom, His immense love, and mercy stir us to deep respect and honour: He is indeed fearsome. This One is unknowable yet discloses Himself to whosoever will come. The Almighty God gently cares for the most fragile, and speaks tenderly to His beloved children.

A Meditation on the Seven Fold Spirit
The following is an example of a time of mediation I spent using the discipline of Listening Prayer or Soaking (see chapter 6).

Rest: As I meditated on the presence of God resting upon me I saw an inner vision of a white feather furled up like a fiddle head fern, as it first appears in spring. As I rested in God's presence the feather unfurled over me reminding me of Psalm 91 (find rest in the shadow of the Almighty). I looked closer at the feather which was configured like a fern leaf. Each part of the fern leaf/feather was an angel equipped and ready to serve me with whatever I need. Thus the thought occurred : God's protection and provision is my shelter. Peace enveloped me as I pondered on His Spirit, who is all I need, resting upon me.

Wisdom: I then asked Holy Spirit to explain His wisdom to me. I saw in the spirit a black MGB sports car. Black symbolizes wisdom in the scripture. In the inner vision I was driving confidently and fast, wearing white driving gloves with tiny holes in them which allows air to flow to the skin. God was saying that wisdom moves ahead fast, as we take hold with a holy and righteous attitude (white symbolizes holiness). Confidence comes as we allow the flow of the spirit to permeate our steering (decision making).

The next thing that happened in this vision was not what I was expecting. The car turned onto a highway merging into a line of traffic. The MGB merged into the middle of a line of other black MGB's moving along the highway. I then understood God was showing wisdom moves in agreement with the wise, not needing to be the first in line or to be more special that those who are moving with Holy Spirit. Living by the Spirit of Wisdom is a higher way of live. (The highway)

Understanding: Next I meditated on the Spirit of

Understanding. Three symbols appeared in order: a plane, a bird, and a Canada goose. Planes fly well, fast, carry lots of weight, but they lack the flexibility I noted in the bird. Birds can change direction with ease and flex their wings, tail and body to do aerial aerobics. Unlike planes, birds can land anywhere they like, rest when they like as long as they like.

The Canada goose, unlike a plane which has to be driven with charts and man-made schedules, instinctively knows the times and seasons for flying. They are at the right place and at the right time of year. The goose is an amazing metaphor for the Spirit of Understanding in that it knows when to wait, nest, molt, and move on. Now that's understanding at a gut level! Contrary to the stereo-type of the "silly goose" the Canada goose displays understanding. It moves long distances in agreement and uniformity with its fellows, enabling even the weakest member's safety and security on the journey. The strength of numbers as well as flexibility of the single bird is combined to display the attribute of understanding.

Many times I have been on auto pilot in my life not attuning to the spontaneous unction's of Holy Spirit, when what I needed was the flexibility like that of a bird to follow Gods current. It is important for me to know the times and seasons in which I live so I will move in agreement with God's plans and with His people. The Spirit of Understanding brings me into the kind of spiritual flight pattern that has been determined by God with which He is imparting to His people in many places at once. Understanding and sensitivity to Holy Spirits direction brings us into unity of the Body of Christ worldwide.

Counsel: The Spirit of Counsel appeared as a piece of chiffon cloth: light as air, translucent, black background with large peach daisy flowered print. The cloth was fashioned into a soft transparent coat. Through this metaphor, I understood God to say that His counsel is transparent, it is unclouded by ulterior motives, with no room for hidden agendas. Those who would counsel others by the Spirit of God must have a life without any hidden motives. What you see is what you get! The counsel they give needs to be lived out in their own lives, producing good things. The black background of the fabric symbolized wisdom being the basis or foundation of our counsel. The peach coloured daisy represents the sweet, fruitful, and uncomplicated words of counsel.

Godly counsel brings simplicity and clarity to circumstances that have been confused and clouded. When the Spirit of Counsel speaks people receive understanding with which to bring resolution (reminds me of a song: "I can see clearly now the rain has gone"). The Spirit of Counsel sweeps in and the fog of confusion lifts.

Might: As I focused on the next aspect of the Holy Spirit, the coat which I was seeing turned into a kimono. I watched as an exhibition of martial arts took place. I thought how graceful the moves were. Full of grace, and yet as God lifted the veil and gave me a glimpse of the unseen spiritual realm I saw the beautiful dance was actually defeating spiritual enemies. What looked at first to be graceful moves were blows that connected in an unseen fight. A spirit war was being fought and won, effortlessly, by Holy Spirit attuned movements. The Spirit of Might is the power of God flowing through His people. The end result is victory over the enemies of God and man. It is the might or strength of God that is unleashed by the Spirit of God to effect spiritual purpose. As Ephesians 6 explains the weapons of our warfare are not carnal (natural or earthly) but are mighty to the pulling down of strongholds. The spirit of might is power to fight the good fight of faith, in alignment with the nature of God. I have learned the weapons of are warfare are actually the fruit of His Spirit listed in Gal 2:20. The ability to wield those weapons comes from the Spirit of Might.

Knowledge of God: Following this I asked God to teach me about knowledge of God I wondered what it might look like to know God and partake of His knowledge. I saw, in vision, a sea-side. The waves came toward me as I sat on the sand. The waves washed up and buffeted me and as I sat there I remembered, from my childhood in Australia, not paying attention while I looked for shells and being bowled over many a time by the force the sea I`d turned my back to. I began to realize what God was saying through this metaphor about the knowledge of God. Truth has a lot to do with knowledge. Truth about God and knowledge of life as He sees it is huge and powerful. Yet if we face it we can be prepared and not be taken by surprise, bowled over, dragged under, or overwhelmed. As with the sea, when we face the waves (truth/knowledge) and step into them we experience an amazing fact: In the deeper waters we are no longer buffeted, as we wade in and get beyond the breakers, we begin to be buoyed up by the smoother rolling waves. The deeper we go (the more we acknowledge truth and agree with God) the gentler the water seems. The knowledge of God /truth about God and life becomes a comfort to us, not harsh reality that seems to buffet and throw us around, but knowledge that brings guidance and lifts us above difficulties to know the truth from God. The knowledge of God brings waves of faith and grace for every potential overwhelming circumstance in life because God`s nature is good, kind generous, merciful and gracious among many other wonderful attributes the knowledge of which is imparted by the Holy Spirit.

Fear of the Lord: As I meditated on the meaning of the sea God moved me onto the next attribute of Holy Spirit: the Fear of the Lord. I was out in the ocean now, far from any land, all I could see was ocean. I dove under and the Holy Spirit took me very deep. I began to see very fearsome creatures of the deep ocean…. fish with lights and huge teeth, dark eerie looking creatures. I could feel sharks and wales swimming above, but then I was reminded this is my Fathers territory and I am in Him, protected and completely safe. I was among His creatures and as a child of God I had dominion over his creation. I felt the peace of knowing the awesomeness of this huge ocean with all its potential to harm me was my playground, and the creatures were friends not matter how fierce they appeared. Daddy was in charge and I was safe in the immense powerful ocean of His presence. I swam even deeper still toward a huge glowing heart. As I approached the heart I could feel it pulsating. It was warm and welcoming, the heart of my Father. I sensed God say the elements in water of Hydrogen 2 parts Oxygen and also Nitrogen stood for the qualities He loves to see in His children…..Honesty, Openness and Obedience and to be Near Him. Then I was drawn into the heart through an artery and He told me there are many chambers in His heart, many more than the human heart. I asked to see into one. He took me into the bridal chamber…which is a metaphor full of meaning

Suggested Meditation or Journaling Exercise

You may like to ask Holy Spirit to speak to you about one of the names or the symbols used to describe His nature. As with the example above you could spend time in Soaking or Listening prayer. Below are sample questions you may like to use.

Holy Spirit please speak to me about the way You show Your life through me, for example how You breathe on me, flow in me, clothe me, etc.

What does it mean that You are the Spirit of the knowledge of God and the fear of the Lord?

Chapter 3 – Holy Spirit the Giver

In general, most people have a good idea, when it comes to human relationships, what to expect; for instance, we usually recognize what is appropriate when hosting with others. We recognize the differing levels of commitment, whether it be hosting a guest for the evening, taking in a boarder or the much deeper level of commitment when entering into marriage. Yet many of us have not given much thought to the design and parameters that God has in mind when we invite His Spirit to come live within us.

When we welcome a friend in our home to dine with us, she may bring a gift to show thanks or good etiquette. Often it is something to share at the table or flowers to bring beauty to it. This custom is lovely – as well as very suitable considering the preparation and resources involved in being hosts. In terms of making a larger commitment, such as the life-changing decision to allow the person to move into our home, we expect them to contribute more than a gesture of thanks.

Many people invite Holy Spirit to come into their lives as an honoured guest. This invitation is nice but not at the same level that Holy Spirit requires. He cannot merely come to visit our home, the human spirit. Holy Spirit must come to dwell in the most all-encompassing way and because of the requirements He has, He cannot simply come as an occasional guest.

The huge provision God has made for us has changed heaven and earth; the magnitude of what this involves is infinitely broader than human etiquette. Since the resurrection of Jesus, God will only send His Spirit to dwell within the human spirit on a permanent basis. No more a visitor, He is now a full-time resident and so the requirements of relationship have a covenant commitment level to them, like marriage. To accommodate the union between Holy Spirit and human, transformation must take place in the human spirit.

The Spirit of God must have a clean and set apart (that is, holy) place where sin cannot occupy any part. Holiness cannot co-habit with uncleanness; such being the case, repentance is essential for the Spirit of God to come into our spirit. At a spirit level every person who has received Holy Spirit is clean regardless of outward appearance. If we have the Spirit of God living within us He has cleansed and made us suitable for His presence. This is a supernatural gift, that God comes to dwell in the very deepest part of us and makes all things new within our spirit.

He not only cleanses us but also changes our nature by moulding and conforming our spirit into His dwelling place, such that we are no longer merely human but now are Sons and Daughters of God. We are new creatures, partakers of the divine nature, one with Jesus Christ in spirit.

Part of the package that comes when we invite Holy Spirit is His nature, fruit and gifts. We have covered His nature in previous chapters; following is some information you may find helpful about the fruit that grows in us and the gifts that we receive when we are permanently united to Christ by His Spirit. The more we commune with Him and yield to His promptings the more established and manifest these wonderful attributes become in us.

Fruit of the Spirit

*But when the Holy Spirit controls our lives, He
will produce this kind of fruit in us: love, joy,
peace, patience, kindness, goodness, faithfulness,
gentleness, and temperance. Here there is no
conflict with the law. (Galatians 5:22-23)*

The fruit of Holy Spirit is that which He produces in us,
because we are His resting place. As we agree with and yield
to His presence within us, Holy Spirit begins to conform us
to the image of Jesus Christ, Holy Spirit being the very Spirit
of Christ. This work of fashioning us in the likeness of Jesus
causes us to display or manifest who Jesus is.

Jesus Christ is the Lover, the Joy-giver, the Prince of
peace, the One Who is patient, kind, good, faithful, gentle, and
in submission to the Father's control. It is not by our human
effort that the fruit of the spirit begin to flow in our lives, it
is by the Holy Spirit's presence, and initiation: "Not by might
nor by power but by My Spirit," says the Lord. (Zechariah 4:6)

In my early days of walking with Jesus I was confused
as I read the Scriptures about the fruit of the Spirit; I
assumed I was responsible for conforming myself to the
image of Christ and evidencing it. I wanted to be loving,
joyful, peaceful, kind, as well as all the other wonderful
characteristics named in Galatians 5:22 but I became
frustrated when, even though I tried my hardest to emulate
them, my life was not very much changed.

I questioned my spiritual advisor about this and I was
told the fruit would come in time. Though I felt a bit better
I now realize I still did not see that this fruit, I wanted to
produce, was the natural outcome of loving and yielding to
Holy Spirit. It is the fruit of God's spirit - my own spirit that
would manifest these things. As I learned to love God and
grow in intimacy with Him His nature of Love, joy peace and
so on would grow and reproduce in my life.

Many years later Holy Spirit taught me how to agree
with and release these things supernaturally from His flow
living within me. This revelation to me has changed the

way I live and has been working change in me so I may live according to His nature and fruit. The fruit of His Spirit are produced by the working of His divine power fused to my weakness, so I cannot boast in my ability or take pride in my goodness but must recognize this fruit is Him living His goodness through me.

A Lesson from the Garden:

Let's ponder the gardening metaphor. As everyone knows if you plant or sew a particular type of seed in the ground it will produce in kind. For example; radish seeds produce radishes. The quality of the fruit and how much is produced is due to natural elements like; rain, temperature, sunlight and soil quality. If all these factors are suitable you will have an abundant yield of radishes. Natural seed produces the type of fruit or vegetable you have sewn and yield is dependent upon varying environmental conditions.

Spiritual fruit grows in a similar way: In the case of spiritual gardening the soil is your soul (mind, will, emotions, conscience, and imagination). The seed is God's word, His essence and nature planted in you through the Holy Spirit. This supernatural seed of the Spirit produces a supernatural crop. Interestingly the amount of supernatural fruit we produce is not dependant upon the elements around as it is with natural seed (rain and sunlight etc.). It does not depend on our soil quality like; if our lives are in perfect order, if our environment is peaceful and conflict free, or even if we are hard working. The crop quality and abundance is due to our willingness to yield. We produce a good crop of spiritual fruit if we will yield to the work the Holy Seed wants to do in us.

We cannot produce supernatural spiritual fruit from natural human seed. If we use love as our example: We desire to love others. If we are to love with God's love we must fuel up or be seeded with the love of God first. We must have the supernatural love of God thriving in us through connecting with God's love in our own hearts. Then we can draw upon that love for others. Otherwise our love will be merely human, natural love, produce by our human effort. We will

be loving with human love, which is nice but far inferior
supernatural.

It takes spiritual seed to produce supernatural fruit.
The fruit of the Spirit is produced by supernatural seeds
from God's nature not from the natural human nature. We
do not expect an apple tree to grow from radish seeds and so
we cannot expect to produce supernatural love from human
sources. *To yield spiritual fruit we must yield our spirit and
soul to God.*

Fruit that Attracts People:

The Fruit of Holy Spirit is the character and nature of God
worked out in us supernaturally by Him. The beauty of the
nature of God in us becomes a magnet which draws people.
The world has nothing in comparison to supernatural love,
joy, peace, patience, gentleness, goodness, faith, humility or
moderation. People long for the peace and joy we embody.
They love to be near us because they notice it in and around
us. So we become magnets for the lost, wounded, and
searching people all around us. They are drawn by Him in us.

I had the experience of being touched physically by
strangers in different situations. People would want to touch
my hair or jewelry or feel the texture of my clothing. It was a
bit uncomfortable for me and I asked the Lord: "What's with
this touching thing God? You know I feel comfortable being
touched by strangers!"

God's reply to me way simple; "They want me Yvonne,
they feel Me in you. I am drawing them. Let it be a signal to
you these ones are being drawn".

Fruit that Repels Evil:

Supernatural attributes are powerful. We see from the word
of God that "the weapons of our warfare are not carnal, but
mighty through God to the pulling down of strong holds"
1 Corinthians 10:4. These weapons we are given are not
obtained or made in natural or carnal way. We cannot
produce weapons that fight our supernatural foe Satan. The
only way to fight evil is with the resources of Heaven.

If we consider our enemies tactics, his weapons that kill, steal and destroy us are things like; hatred, depression, rage, impatience, violence, lust, doubt, pride and addiction to name just a few. However, we see in a list of God's characteristics His fruit is the anti-dote for everything evil can use to harm us. His fruit is the antidote for the negative feelings that attack our soul. When we are filled with Holy Spirit, there is no room for strongholds of evil: Jesus our deliverer casts out our enemies.

For example:

- God's love cancels out hatred in our hearts, it drives out fear that probably caused hate.

- The joy of the Lord strengthens us to rise up against things like depression. Joy is God's clam delight as well as happiness.

- The peace of God quells rage and guards our hearts and minds as well.

- God's patience in our hearts overrides Satan's striving and impatience.

- Supernatural gentleness stands firm against violence. A gentle answer turns away wrath.

- The goodness of God leads us to repentance and integrity deals with dishonesty and sin.

- The faith of God moves enemy mountains of doubt and unbelief.

- Meekness or humility keeps us close to the heart of God so pride has no place.

- Holy Spirit control keeps our desires, needs, and passions in moderation and balance.

Against such amazing weapons there is no evil equal. No law of God will limit the amounts of such beautiful characters to be displayed and released through our lives each day. We can be sure these divine characteristics are heavens answer to bring hells strategies to naught. We need these attributes of God today in our hearts as well as out in the world. We who have the Holy Spirit living in our spirit have all we need for life and godliness all we need to do is agree with God and yield.

Suggested Meditation or Journaling Exercise
Lord please speak to me about Your fruit in my life.

What do You want to say to me about bearing fruit?

Gifts of the Spirit

When we consider what the early church experienced, we see the extremes of their circumstances as exciting as well as dangerous - how those who were with Jesus must have felt at His arrest, trial, conviction, execution and then the amazing resurrection, supernatural appearances and ascension. After such astounding occurrences they were told to wait for the promised power to come[12].

We see from the book of Acts that these early believers surely did receive the empowerment of Holy Spirit because they evidenced radical change in their boldness for God and in their ability to perform many wondrous supernatural acts. It is easy to see the difference these special abilities made in their lives. As we live in times that seem increasingly extreme, the use of all of God's precious gifts are just as relevant and needed.

Following are various biblical examples of the empowerment God provides by Holy Spirit.

- **Prophecy:** According to Luke 1:67, Zechariah, the father of John the Baptist, was filled by Holy Spirit to give prophecy.

- **Languages, eloquence and boldness:** According to Acts 2:4, 7, 8, 11, 31, and 33, the disciples were empowered and enabled to testify about Christ,

---

12   Acts1: 4-8

declaring the wonders of God.

- **Performing miracles:** According to Acts 19:11, God did extraordinary miracles through the apostle Paul.

- **Spiritual vision to see God's Glory:** According to Acts 7:55, Stephen at his martyrdom saw the heavens open and the Glory of God was revealed to him. This gave him supernatural grace and forgiveness that witnessed to all those who saw his boldness in the face of death.

- **Discernment:** According to Acts 13:9-19, Paul, who was filled with the Holy Spirit, looked straight at Elymas the Sorcerer and said, "You are a child of the devil". Jesus also exercised discerning of spirits, as in Mark 2:8.

- **Giving hope:** According to Romans 15:13, the power of the Holy Spirit brought the early church to overflow with supernatural hope in extremely difficult circumstances.

- **Demonstrations of power:** According to 1Corinthians 2:4, Paul's messages were validated by demonstrations of God's power.

- **Inner strengthening:** In Ephesians 3:5, Paul prays for others to be strengthened inwardly by Holy Spirit just as he had experienced.

This power (Greek dunamis) is resident in Holy Spirit and continues among us today. As we invite Him to fill us and yield to His greatness we will also be endowed with this same dunamis power.

Three Types of Gifts

Scripture provides three different lists of the gifts or special abilities that come with the Holy Spirit. The compilation of the lists from these scriptures is as follows: Administration,

Apostle, Discerning of Spirits, Encouraging, Evangelist, Faith, Giving, Healing, Mercy, Miracles, Pastor, Prophecy, Service, Teaching, Tongues, Word of Knowledge and Word of Wisdom The gifts are given in three separate lists for purpose. Scripture gives clarity as to the reason the lists are arranged differently. 1 Corinthians 12:4-6 breaks down the differences:

- There are different kinds of gifts, but the same Spirit. (KJV: gifts)

- There are different kinds of service, but the same Lord. (KJV: administrations)

- There are different kinds of working but the same God works all of them in all men. (KJV: operations)

Different kinds of gifts: Described in 1 Corinthians 14:14 (Greek word for gifts here is charisma) this list refers to the supernatural manifestations produced by Holy Spirit including: healing miracles, languages, and prophecy these gifts are used to minister to others in the power of Holy Spirit. The second 1 Corinthians passage describes the correct use of these supernatural gifts.

Different kinds of service: Described in Ephesians 4:7-13 (Greek word for service or operations is diakonia) this list refers to the leadership roles which enable the body of Christ to learn, grow, and be nurtured into maturity. This list, known as the fivefold ministry gifts, includes: Apostle, Prophet, Pastor, Evangelist, and Teacher.

Different kinds of working: Described in Romans 12:6-8 (Greek meaning of working or operations is dore to move as time moves) this list refers to the gift God gives which moves or motivates us to act. This list is made of some of the gifts within the other lists and includes: prophecy, serving, teaching, encouraging, giving, leading, and mercy. We will begin our exploration of the gifts in detail by looking at the motivational gifts.

The Motivational Gifts

God has given each of us a heart motivation which will align us with His purpose for our life; that we will fit beautifully into his plans meshing with the body of Christ. The motivational gift is given before we are born and is part of our spiritual DNA. We may notice it before we come to know God. It is often evident in early childhood. When we give our lives to Jesus Christ and receive the Holy Spirit the motivational gift blossoms, heightens and grows as we mature in God. Other gifts (supernatural gifts) come as we yield and are filled by Holy Spirit. These are called manifestational gifts because they are an outward working of Holy Spirit as He manifests through us. It is helpful to know the motivational gift directs or impassions us to act in certain ways much like our personality. In fact the gift that motivates us is an integral part of who we are causing us to view life and people through its particular lens. Following is a description of the motivational gifts along with characters including positive and negative aspects.

Prophet: Always passionate for truth the prophet will not compromise the word of God. Those who are motivated by the gift of prophet are ready to move when God is moving. They are positioned ahead of people calling them to follow what the Lord is about to do. Prophets are often loners spending many hours with God even preferring solitary life. The Prophet delights in bringing people into Holiness and alignment with God's truth. The downside to this gift is that prophets can be harsh or blunt with words and can be at times too insistent that people act on the words they have delivered. Prophets can be tempted to bitterness and offence if people do not receive truth or correction.

Server: These helpful people love to care for and meet physical needs so as to enable others to fulfill their mandate. They enjoy doing practical things. Their motivation is to pitch in and make things happen. The server is a team player who loves people and enjoys the fellowship of working for a common purpose. Godly Servers live with integrity. Their deepest desire is to enable others to prosper. They are generally selfless, hard-working and quick to volunteer. The downside of this gift is that they can be easily ignored and or victimized by those who will overload them. They need to follow the unction of Holy Spirit and do as Jesus did in their serving (He did only the will of His Father).

Teacher: Teachers love to study, research, and impart truth. They lay a foundation of biblical principles for practical application. Teachers instruct from researched and proven sources. They discern what needs to be corrected in order to alleviate problems. Teachers tend not to be social and relational unless they see a practical purpose in it. They may be people who are content in solitude and study. The teacher prepares the Body of Christ by giving a solid foundation of truth which others can build upon. Teachers can become stuck in dogma and hair splitting over small issues (pharisaical spirit). They may lack in relational building skills. Teachers may also find research fills hours of time to the detriment of time spent with God enjoying relationship with Him.

Encourager: This gift brings people along in their journey of faith. Those whose motivation is to encourage brings hope for the future to the Body of Christ which enables people to go on into their calling. The Encourager can be an excellent exhorter, preacher and teacher using personal testimony stories. Not afraid of preaching to the crowd, often the encourager becomes the life of the party. They can find time management and personal retreat a challenge because of this tendency toward the company of people rather than focusing their attention on solitary tasks. Spending quality, alone time with God can also be a challenge for them. Encouragers can be tempted to live in rejection or the fear of it. They can be prone to people please to gain acceptance.

Giver: The resource people, givers love to help people fulfill their kingdom purpose. They often give from their own finances but also connect people with resources from other places. Givers are independent and self-motivated. They think long term and look at the investment value in their giving. Givers need to learn to be discerning in giving; to be generous but not indiscriminate. The biggest challenge for the giver is to give from faith not only from their own resources, but from the heart of God. Intimacy with God can be an issue for the giver so often God uses the need for wisdom in giving to draw them into closer communion.

Leader: This gift brings teams of people together for common purpose. Leaders see the big picture and desire to release heaven`s plans upon the earth. They have many kingdom ideas and much vision. A leader is not usually one to volunteer but will rise up into potential if called upon. They need the focus of God to narrow their sights and fulfill their part of a project. A leader is good at organizing all the pieces of a project but not always good at seeing it through to completion. The down side of the Leader gift is that they can go ahead of God as well as others acting too quickly. Leaders need to learn dependence upon God, to learn to honour God through their obedience in seeking Him and waiting for His timing.

Mercy: The person motivated by Mercy is the lover of the body of Christ. They nurture, reassure, and bring healing to broken hearted. Mercy gift fits well with every gift because mercy brings the heart of God into the equation. Mercy can see both sides of the issue which can also cause the Mercy giver to hold back correction when it is needed. These people team wonderfully with the teacher, prophet or leader who may not be as apt to feel the compassion of God for His people. The down side for the Mercy giver is they tend not to stand on values but to people please for acceptance. They can be tempted to keep peace instead of mercifully speaking truth. Mercy givers need to learn from Jesus to stand in truth but deliver it in love, being steadfast in truth and grace. Holy Spirit, speak to me about the gifts You have given me. What gift have you given me to motivate me to minister?

The Manifestational Gifts

The first listing of gifts noted in the 1 Corinthians 12:4-6 passage is referring to the charisma or supernatural manifestations of the Spirit. These gifts or abilities empower us to minister in the revelations and miracles of God. All of the gifts noted in these three lists can be manifested through us when needed. Most believers move in one or two regularly and become confident in their operation through them. For example one may be born with the gift of mercy but often is able to move in prophetic words of knowledge and healing. The specific list of healing, miracles, languages and prophecy are abilities which only operate through the power of God and cannot be worked through human resources. Other gifts can be used through our natural resources and supernatural unction such as; teaching, serving, giving, encouraging, administration, mercy, apostle, pastor, and evangelist. It is important to note: though we may be able to perform these functions in our natural abilities we will not be moving in agreement with God's preference which is that we operate in and through Holy Spirit's unction and power. This is accomplished by continually yielding to Him, inviting Him to speak, and receiving His direction in our operation in these abilities and functions.

Healing: All healing comes from God. Healing can be physical, emotional, or spiritual and in each of those areas God is the healer. Supernatural healing is more overtly a work of God as the scripture says it is a normal activity of those who follow Jesus[13]. There are many examples of the disciples of Jesus working healing miracles. Usually miracles of healing are outstanding such as bones mending or realigning instantly, pain instantly leaving, cancers leaving the body, as well as long standing illnesses or diseases being cured rapidly etc.

Miracles: Jesus performed many miracles where He caused the forces of nature to work counter to natural order[14]. The early believers did likewise and many people in our day have had the privilege of doing the same by God's supernatural power.

Languages: This supernatural gift comes in the

---

13   Mark 16:17 & 18
14   Jesus walks on water: John14:25, Feeds four thousand: John15:32-38

speaking of unknown (to the speaker) languages often called the gift of Tongues and also interpretation of tongues. The languages can be in earthly and heavenly languages[15]. This supernatural ability is given to edify our own spirit by aligning our inner-man toward the Holy Spirit. It is also a sign to others that God is at work especially if the language is earthly and understood by them. I have spoken in Bengali a language I do not naturally speak or understand. The woman who told me was new to the gifts of the Spirit and also beginning to learn Bengali to better help the people she had been winning to Christ. She interpreted the language I was using at the time as a phrase in Bengali meaning; "To the beautiful One, the beautiful one who is among us". I was very blessed to be told what I had been singing and she was reassured that the gift of tongues or prayer language is from the Lord. She had naturally interpreted what she had learned. However, there is also the gift of interpretation.

Interpretation of languages in its supernatural form can come through inner-knowing where one receives the overall understanding of what God is saying and can explain the overall meaning. It can also come as phrases of English, in the thoughts of the listener, whilst the speaker is talking in the unknown language. Language can also be interpreted prophetically by the next prophetic utterance that follows. The person who speaks in the tongue may receive the interpretation, or any person present may be given the interpretation.

Prophecy (Word of Knowledge & Wisdom): These gifts of the Holy Spirit are known as Revelatory Gifts, meaning they supernaturally reveal things not naturally known.

Spending time in God's presence will transition us into His supernatural gifts and abilities. As we mature in agreement with God, listen for His voice, commune with Him daily, and act on His promptings the revelatory gifts of Holy Spirit will become stronger within us.

My experience with these abilities began after I was initially filled with the Spirit of God. As I devoted myself to

---

15   1 Corinthians 13:1

Jesus, communing with Him each day, I began to receive words of knowledge as well as understanding or wisdom. This first happened while praying for others, and later I received knowledge of things I could not humanly know spontaneously, without any effort or prayer on my part. I did not ask for this knowledge, these revelatory events came both spontaneously, when I was in prayer for others, and during listening prayer times.

I have discovered some helpful tips on my own learning curve I trust the following information assist you in your journey.

Word of Knowledge

Supernatural knowledge is basically information that is planted in me. This knowledge may come to me as soon as I begin to think of praying for the person or situation. It can come through a sense of touch, taste, smell, vision or thought.

My experience with word of knowledge is that information I do not naturally know is just there, in my mind, usually before I even have a chance to look for Jesus or to hear God's voice with regards to a person. Knowledge can be imparted through all of our senses as well as emotions.

Using Word of Knowledge as a Ministry Tool

As I have mentioned, a word of knowledge feels like I already "knew", although there is no natural way I would have had access to the information. I then talk to the Lord about it, asking Him whether I should share it as it is (raw, so to speak). According to His prompting, I may share it uninterpreted (e.g. "I see a black dog bearing its teeth. Have you encountered such an animal in your life?") The recipient can then confirm whether this was indeed a word of knowledge (e.g. "My aunt has a black dog, and it tried to bite me last month.") At that point, I am free to go on with what the Lord is saying for them, having perhaps now established a better connection with the individual.

This approach allows the prophetic word which may follow a greater likelihood of being well received: the word of knowledge came first, showing that God really knows about the recipients' life, cares about them, and wants to communicate with them through us.

On the other hand, if the revelation does not appear to be a word of knowledge (e.g. "No, that doesn't ring a bell, I haven't had an encounter with a black dog"), then we have the opportunity, as God leads, to give interpretation to the metaphor, as in the following section.

Word of Wisdom

While basic wisdom is the application of knowledge and experience, supernatural wisdom involves interpretation and application given from God, not from human thinking. Sometimes without natural knowledge or experience, we just sense how to handle a situation thanks to direction and insights that are from God. Supernatural wisdom is delivered to us Spirit to spirit, not from our natural reasoning or experience but from God's unlimited resources.

A word of wisdom very often arises like a word of knowledge, in that we already seem to "know"; with a word of wisdom, Holy Spirit provides guidance regarding how to put the revelation into practice, so that, we will know God's direction as to what to do in a particular situation. Even if we lack the information that human decision-making would require. Word of wisdom gives us confidence to act or to give counsel to another.

At times I have experienced this download of supernatural wisdom and, without realizing what had happened, began to speak wise words from Holy Spirit.

Using Word of Wisdom as a Ministry Tool

When God is giving wisdom, it is almost always something we could not have devised in human thinking. I have often experienced God's wisdom flow from my mouth as I teach, God providing practical application (for example, meeting specific individual needs which I may only learn of later). This supernatural flow of wisdom unlocks people's circumstances and brings to their lives God's anointed strategy and action plans.

There are occasions when we receive wisdom with time to ask the Lord about it, and wait for His response before we release words as His counsel. At these moments, it seems the timing of delivering this wisdom is important: if it is for us to deliver to someone else, we need to ask for the appropriate opportunity to speak it. When a word of wisdom is given for our own personal circumstances, we need to ask God for the right time to put it into action.

Allow me to again stress the difference between good advice and the revelatory gift that is a word of wisdom. Although good advice can be godly and helpful, it is not supernaturally downloaded or discerned; it comes by experience and knowledge, so it is natural. While this does not necessarily make it bad or wrong, it is just not the same as a word of wisdom from Holy Spirit.

Human wisdom can sometimes cloud issues and even cause the revelatory prophetic word to become lost in the fog of too much information. Caution must be used especially in group settings: too much information can cause confusion. Confusion is a demonic spirit; not at all helpful for those listening for God's words to them. God will give clarity - the enemy attempts to muddy the waters of understanding. Supernatural wisdom brings clarity, peace and an action plan.

Prophecy

When our heart is connected to the heart of Jesus it allows us to feel the love of God towards the one for whom we are prophesying.

In my experience a prophetic word often comes when I am praying for a person, as I focus on Jesus and listen to God with regards to the person or situation: prophecy follows as I simply pass on to others what the Lord is saying to me.

The prophecy may come in the form of words, pictures, impressions or some other voice God wants to use at the time[16]. Our part is to be open and sensitive to the Spirit of God within us. The words that flow from a spirit filled with

_____
16   See Chapter 5 "How God Speaks"

the love and grace of God will be more effective and healing. On the other hand, if we are struggling to love the recipient, we need to be quiet; any revelation we have for that person may be tainted by our personal opinion or some judgment or offence we are carrying in their regard.

Of course, if we are speaking in the name of God, we need to exercise care! The Spirit of Prophecy is the Spirit of Jesus so we need to be very close to Him, manifesting His love, truth and peace, if we are to impart His heart to others.

Using Prophecy as a Ministry Tool

When operating in the gift of Prophecy we need to remember some that people do not understand prophecy or are offended by it. I usually first seek God for direction and wisdom as to how I should proceed with what He has given me for them. It is best to ask God whether or not we are to share at all, as well as what to share – perhaps just a portion of the bigger picture we have seen is to be communicated. Sometimes, we need to pray into the revelation without necessarily speaking it out loud at all. Other times we turn the prophecy into a prayer. For example "Thank You Lord Jesus that you have good relationships for our sister here and you are going to give her wisdom as to who to trust and who she needs to be careful around. Lord bless her with wisdom and understanding and protect her from negative relationships. Lord alert her about negative talk and keep her from harmful words. I pray that no weapon formed against her will prosper and every word spoken against her will not prosper." This prayer would be helpful if you had seen the black dog bearing its teeth (interpretation - a friend who is not friendly but ready to take a verbal piece out of the person)

Understanding the Differences

Every child of God has the equipment to receive messages from God and has the ability to commune with Him. God loves to even share the secrets of His heart with His children and we need to honour, value and desire what our Father wants to communicate. He will increase our desire for intimacy, but He also wants to see if we will come to Him in love, just to spend time loving Him in return. This reciprocal love relationship is the fertile ground for supernatural growth. God will give us more in the area of revelation as we mature in our love for Him.

We need to understand a little about the differences between these areas of revelation. If we do not distinguish between Word of Knowledge and Prophecy, for instance, we may make the mistake of prophesying something that may be a desire of a human heart and not what God is saying He would do. For example, a couple desiring to have a child may come for prayer. If we are not careful to discern, we may think that the baby we are seeing is what God has for them; we may however be picking up on their desire which would be a Word of Knowledge. If that were the case, the couple could be very disappointed, had we "prophetically" told them that God showed us a baby in their future, and yet that did not come to pass.

We also need to discern the difference between a Word of Wisdom and earthly wisdom or good advice so we are assured we are speaking on behalf of God and not from our own resources. God is wonderful at fulfilling His word, much more so than we can be at following through on our own advice; therefore, we need to learn the difference. Once we are assured we have a word of wisdom we need to talk to the Lord about the timing whether it is for the moment of future disclosure.

To summarize the difference between prophecy and word of wisdom: Prophecy is God speaking to a person through another (the prophet) where as Word of wisdom is God's application and strategy for accomplishing something that we otherwise did not have a plan of action for.

The process for me in receiving revelation may not be exactly the same as it is for you as we are all made so wonderfully unique. In any case, we can trust our Maker to teach us discernment through our relationship with Him. The ministry of Holy Spirit is to teach and train, which He does uniquely for all.

A practical example of the use of the revelatory gifts: The Lord may prompt me to interpret the Word of Knowledge, rendering it prophetic (e.g. "I see a black dog bearing its teeth. Could this represent a friend turning on you, not deserving the trust you have had in him or her?") Note the difference here: The prophetic rendition interprets the message rather than asking if the person has the black dog in their history. Here too, the recipient can respond as to whether this applies to them or not, with the potential of a greater opportunity for me to move forward with speaking on behalf of Holy Spirit for the individual (i.e. "God wants you to know that He...")

Then perhaps a word of wisdom will follow such as: "God is impressing that this person is wounded and needs understanding, that you need to set safe boundaries for yourself, keep the relationship open but some distance is needed to keep it healthy."

Suggested Meditation or Journaling Exercise

Holy Spirit what do you want to say to me about your revelatory gifts?

The Five-Fold Administrative Gifts

The list of service or administrative gifts names both anointing or abilities and serving positions in the body of Christ are Apostle, Prophet, Evangelist, Pastor and Teacher. These abilities are for the benefit of God's people to build them up and mentor them into greater confidence in the Spirit. Holy Spirits noticeable work in and through us, so that we are able to operate in supernatural abilities, is often called "The Anointing".

The Apostle: This is a gifting that breaks new ground, starts new things, and implements strategies for God's kingdom to increase in areas where darkness pervaded. The anointing to take ground in new areas is an ability which can be used in the body of Christ, in business, in the arts, in government, in technology and more. This ability can be seen even in the secular world, for example; successful businesses whose leaders begin ground breaking work. People who make huge gains in technological areas which change the lives of many are Apostolic.

These Apostolic gifts are God given whether they are used for His kingdom or not. God's people who are gifted to break new ground and orchestrate new kingdom strategies are often accompanied by signs, wonders, and miracles which authenticate their gifting. These supernatural acts create an environment of faith where other believers can be confident to join the team to accomplish the large tasks God has called the Apostle to do. Apostles often birth large movements of God which bring God's kingdom into new levels of recognition and accomplishment in which God is given honour and glory. The large scope and big picture of the Apostle needs to be tempered by the humility of Christ and patience for those who may be slow to act on the direction of Holy Spirit.

The Prophet: as mentioned is a gift of discerning the word of the Lord, which can come through any or all of the senses, (see Chapter 5) and also making God's word known. It is a gift which enables us to hear God for our own edification, encouragement, and comfort as well as to direct us personally. The anointing rests upon every believer, though we do not all move in prophecy often for others. The Prophetic person brings encouragement, edification, and comfort to those to whom the Spirit directs weather they are Christian or not.

The administrative Prophet is one who is accurate in predictive in revelatory prophecy. The Prophet is enabled by the Spirit to supernaturally impart the prophetic gift and mentor others in prophecy. The Prophet's heart is passionate for the truth of the word of the Lord to be followed. The prophet needs to drink of the love and mercy of Jesus and to move in grace for others who may be slow to act upon prophetic direction.

The Evangelist: is the gift which draws those who do not know Jesus Christ into the knowledge of God and relationship with His Spirit. All Christians can operate in the ability to evangelize by the Spirits power but some of us are supernaturally enabled to evangelize with the result that many people are drawn to the truth of knowing God. The Evangelist carries the anointing to lead people to Jesus easily.

A more notable degree of this anointing is that the Evangelist carries the ability to impart the anointing of evangelism to others who then become magnets for hungry seekers who are led to Christ. Evangelists love non-Christians into the kingdom of heaven. They are often more comfortable in the company of non-believers than in they are in church because their gift is not for within the body, but to reach out into the world rescuing the lost. They may not understand the need to nurture and encourage believers because God has given them a huge passion to reach out. Evangelists can become impatient with those who are not passionate for the lost or for the other giftings which minister to those already churched.

The Pastor: This gift of the Spirit cares for, loves, and nurtures the people of God. Pastors are the tenders of God's garden. They are characterized by; strong relational gifts, and gracious perseverance with the imperfections of the growing body of believers. Many of God's people carry the pastoring anointing and love to care for and nurture people. They love to visit the sick and encourage people with acts of kindness, which is God's heart for all his people. Pastoring is not limited to caring for God's household of faith. Many with evangelistic leanings love to pastor those who are not yet believers. It is thus through the love and care of the pastoring gift that many people believe in the love of God seeing the people of God as their new family and place of belonging.

The gift becomes the administration or leadership ability when the pastor is reproducing those who pastor. The administration to reproduce loving shepherds of God frock is supernaturally imparted. Pastors create a community of God around them much like the "magnetic' effect that the evangelist carries for non-believers. The difficulty for Pastors is where the line is between pastoring from the supernatural anointing and human love and compassion. Burn out occurs when the supernatural is supplanted by human effort in loving and caring for people. When Holy Spirit is leading and empowering much less natural activity is seen however God's kingdom is being produced and flourishing as a result.

The Teacher: The administrative gift of teacher carries all the attributes of the teacher mentioned in the manifestational gift listing as well as the ability to impart the gift and passion of teaching, receiving revelation, and researching to others. The teacher is like the other administrative giftings, a foundation builder of the body of Christ.

Teachers keep believers on track and aligned with the scriptures and the nature and character of God. They often have the ability to discern issues which could erode the foundation of truth and bring clarity to root problems. They are able to; explain and encourage, correcting, and bringing more understanding of how truth can be applied. The teacher in this capacity often has the larger aspect of the Kingdom of God to release, bringing the people of God into agreement with the plans and blue prints of heaven.

Suggested Meditation or Journaling Exercise

Holy Spirit what gift or gifts are good for me to desire and lean about?

Where do I fit in the area of fivefold administrative gifts?

Chapter 4 – Positioned to Receive

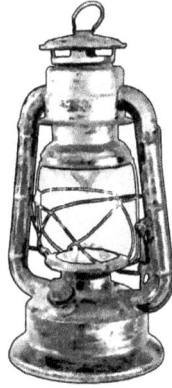

God loves relationship, and He continually desires to communicate with us; therefore, He has established a Spirit-to-spirit union with those who are born into His family. Through receiving His Holy Spirit we are given a new life in spirit. In this "newborn" spiritual life, we are no longer merely human; we are now children of God with a new nature. In fact, the Scripture tells us that the old nature has passed away and the new divine nature has come. We each must learn to live from our new nature.

As children learn from their parents to eat, talk, walk and interact in their physical life, so we, God's children, must also learn from our heavenly parent how to partake and interact in spiritual life, both with Him and the world around us.

In order to learn the spiritual lessons our Father desires us to learn, we must position ourselves to receive from Him. The Triune God (Father, Son, and Holy Spirit) is our parent, teacher, counsellor and so much more. All wisdom and understanding come from Him. As we come, childlike, to learn from Him we mature into sons and daughters who know His heart and carry out His kingdom plans. The Spirit of God deposits God's spiritual DNA into us so this process works according to His design, not our striving.

In my journey of learning, I have found that there are three essential keys which position people to receive from God. They are: where we focus our attention, our understanding of faith in action, and living from the daily filling of Holy Spirit.

Focus

We are commanded to fix our eyes upon Jesus, the author and perfecter of our faith. The Greek word aphorao for "fix our eyes" means to literally view with undivided attention by looking away from every other object. The product of focus is that we become what we focus upon, rather like the sayings, "You are what you eat" and "what you see is what you get". It makes perfect sense, then: since God desires that we become like His beloved Son, He commands us to fix our eyes (give all of our focus to) Jesus. Not only figuratively but physically we benefit from fixing our eyes on Him.

Allow me to explain how one can figuratively and physically focus on Jesus. Jesus only did what He saw His Father do and heard His Father say[17]. If we follow His example, we will learn to do the same. He lived on both sides of the spiritual veil, the heavenly and earthly at one time. It is our privilege and position to do the same because we have been given the same nature and relationship as co-heirs with Jesus Christ[18].

Jesus exemplifies living from divine nature; we may follow His example as we yield our lives and give God our full focus. Jesus physically fixed His inner eyes and ears on the Father who was in heaven to see and hear what Father wanted Him to do. Figuratively Jesus focused his attention and tuned His mind, will, emotions, conscious and imagination on doing what He knew was the Fathers desire. Jesus knew His Father's heart because as a man He learned from the Scriptures just as we have to learn about God. The other side of Jesus relationship was the daily connection through looking and listening actively each day.

It is not only our minds which refocus our attention

---

17 John 5:19-20
18 Colossians3:1-3

to Jesus: we also align and direct our senses toward Him, including our emotions. As we attune to Jesus we will "hear" God with all of our selves. Just like children who learn to focus their natural senses to understand and learn of the world around them, we must learn to attune our spiritual senses to learn what God wants to teach us about spiritual world around us.

Much curiosity and hunger is stirring in our day for spiritual experience. Many are dabbling in supernatural encounters; it needs to be noted, however, that God has given order and instruction that Jesus Christ is the gatekeeper: He is the only way to the Father and those who try to enter by means other than His Son are thieves and robbers (illegal in their entrance), as stated in John 10:6-10.

By contrast, those who are sons and daughters by the blood of Jesus Christ are seated already in heavenly realms so they have permission to enter into His throne room and come boldly before His throne of grace[19].

There is no other way to receive permission; authentic spiritual encounter is only possible for those who have the indwelling Holy Spirit as their interpreter and guide. Warning is clear to those who would trespass; deception is very close at hand for those who ignore the gatekeeper. Those who enter in by the Gate are His own sheep and will hear His voice and not be led astray by the voice of a stranger. This guarantee for knowing the true voice is only for those who know Jesus Christ.

As I focus my attention (all of my faculties) on Jesus, He reveals truth to me. The mysteries of the Kingdom are revealed to the childlike who focus on Jesus and agree with His heart. Focus on Jesus physically (by looking and listening) as well as figuratively (by knowing His nature and heart) is a key which unlocks God's Kingdom flow in and through our lives.

Suggested Meditation or Journaling Exercise
Father please speak to me about my need to focus.

---

19   Ephesians2:6

Holy Spirit please speak to me about improving my focus on Jesus.

Faith

According to the Scriptures, without faith it is impossible to please God[20]. It is by faith that we step into God: without knowing all the answers, we believe God and move forward. Just as we are "saved" or brought into relationship with the Godhead by putting our trust in the price Jesus Christ paid for our redemption, we step into all of the benefits of that redemption by faith.

What is it To Live By Faith?

Perhaps we could answer that question by examining what it looks like when persons, while believing in Jesus, do not live by faith. These individuals in theory believe yet live a natural lifestyle. Decisions are based on human reasoning and human resources.

Without moving in faith, often people will pray for God's wisdom but don't believe He will speak personally to them to impart it. So they continue on in reasoned assessment of their situation, hoping for the best and asking God to bless what they have decided to do.

We can go on our entire lives assuming we are living by faith in the lifestyle I have alluded to - I did just that for twenty years! However, faith without works (action) is dead[21]. Of course God can and does intervene to change, direct and correct our course even though we may not listen to Him. His grace covers many of our mistakes however active faith, by contrast, assumes God is interested, listening, and will not only communicate His desire to us, but direct and manage the outcome of each facet of practical living.

A personal example of this kind of relationship would be my relationship to the Prime Minister of Canada: I opted,

---

20   Hebrews 11:6
21   James 2:26

through citizenship, to become a Canadian; as such I respect and honour Prime Minister. I obey, to the best of my abilities, the laws of his dominion and read his comments or watch and listen to his broadcasts. However, though I may like him, I really do not love him or communicate with him personally. Though I would not break the laws of the land he rules, I never expect him to take part in my personal decisions, or that he would have a plan that I could chat over with him. This is close to what my relationship with God was like for those many years of unfulfillment in my initial walk with Him.

Faith in Action

Someone who is living a life of faith grows in practicing the presence of Jesus Christ. Just as in any healthy relationship communication comes from both parties, so that each one knows what the other likes, and dislikes. The communication grows deeper as more time is granted to it, even to the point of understanding what the other's inner desires, hopes, and future plans involve. The relationship is one of love and commitment where each person becomes vitally interested and contingent to the outworking of life together. When faith is lived out, the two – the individual person and God - become one. The person lives in and through inner union with God, as made possible by the indwelling presence of Holy Spirit.

Spirit-to-spirit connection with God is the birthright of every born-again believer! This life of union with God is similar to an excellent, loving, marriage: each partner is living with and is in daily, loving communication with the other. Each one honours the personhood of the other, desiring only the best and acting in respect toward each other. Their life is shared, and the relationship gives birth to the joint hopes, desires and plans. This is what faith in action looks like. Here in our earthly lives, God has made it possible to enjoy divine union with Himself by the connection of our human spirit with His Holy Spirit.

It is only possible to live our lives in union with God by His power and on His terms. Galatians 2:20 gives us a glimpse of what this encompasses: I have been crucified with

Christ; it is no longer I who live, but Christ lives in me; and the life which I now in the flesh (on earth) live I live by faith in the Son of God, Who loved me and gave Himself for me. A dead person cannot make decisions, evaluate with their own reason, or act on any impulse, desire, or need. We are not physically dead – in our dead-to-self-yet-alive-in-God state, we need to purpose to yield our human resources to the divine nature with which we have been impregnated. Then we will be living according to the verse from Galatians.

By faith we activate our new life, as we follow the lead of the indwelling Holy Spirit and live through His direction, power, and love. As we give permission by choosing to turn to Him and not our own resources, we fulfill God's purposes and bring Him glory enabling Him to accomplish impossible supernatural things through our lives[22].

Suggested Meditation or Journaling Exercise
Holy Spirit, how would You have me grow in exercising faith?

Filled With the Spirit

In writing on the topic of being filled with Holy Spirit I realize there are many differing opinions along with perhaps hundreds of books written, so I will attempt to keep the topic short and hopefully sweet.

Some History
The fulfillment of Jesus' promise: And now I will send the Holy Spirit just as my Father promised. But stay here in the city till the Holy Spirit comes and fills you with power from heaven. (Luke 24:49)

But you will receive power when the Holy Spirit comes upon you and you will be My witnesses, telling people about Me everywhere.... (Acts 1:8)

The promise of Jesus to His disciples was to give them the Holy Spirit who would release in them same power He

---

22   Mark 9:29

had. This power enables us to perform supernatural acts and tell people everywhere of the grace and mercy of God. It enables us to have not only forgiveness and access to God but also to be made new creatures through union with the Holy Spirit. This enablement is what each person is given when they believe in Jesus' power to forgive through His death, burial, and resurrection. When people believe and invite Holy Spirit into their lives they receive a new nature, that of being eternally united with God. A new creature is formed: the old nature is past and the new has begun[23].

The first instance of Spirit infilling: We often think of the passage in Acts 2:1-4, as the first occurrence of Holy Spirit coming to the newly founded church, however, there is an earlier time when the believers were given the Spirit. It was the evening of the first day of His resurrection (after Mary's encounter near the tomb) the Scriptures tell us Jesus appeared to the disciples gathered behind locked doors[24]. He told them that He was sending them in the same way the Father had sent him, then He breathed on them and said: "Receive the Holy Spirit." The way God sent the Son was through the connection and empowerment of Holy Spirit and though they did believe in Jesus, they had not been empowered for intimate connection. The breath of Christ gave them the missing element that would release them from cowering in fear (an appropriate human reaction given that the Romans and Sanhedrin would have killed them) into courageous faith.

Now further on in the story, after the ascension, we read of how the Spirit came visibly as tongues of fire lighting upon the heads of each believer, and audibly with the utterance of languages not native to the speakers[25]. This amazing display of power from God was effective in bringing many people who were present to belief in God. After this powerful impartation of the Spirit by God, we see the practice of imparting the Spirit through the hands of those who were first sovereignly filled at the original event.

---

23   2 Corinthians 5:17
24   John 20:19-22
25   Acts2:1-4

These occurrences ushered in a huge shift in the activity of Holy Spirit who, prior to this time, moved occasionally upon singular people or groups of prophets. From this point on we note Holy Spirit coming upon all believers to impart special supernatural gifts. In this first instance, the evidences of the Spirit's work seems to be an impartation of faith. Note: Tomas who was not there did not believe till he saw[26].

At the occasion in Acts 2: 1-4 we notice the impartation produced supernatural power in the form of tongues or languages unknown to the speakers (but recognized as native to the hearers) and also a new boldness and clarity in preaching the gospel of Christ. Later the disciples now called Apostles began to do the supernatural works Jesus had done.

The laying on of hands and prayer: (Acts 8:15-17) "As soon as they arrived, they prayed for these new believers to receive the Holy Spirit. The Holy Spirit had not yet come upon any of them, for they had only been baptized in the name of the Lord Jesus. Then Peter and John laid hands upon these believers, and they received the Holy Spirit."

The laying on of hands by those who had already received Holy Spirit continued to be practiced thereafter. We do not read of anyone not receiving who was thus prayed for, and it seems many if not all received a supernatural language which they (the speakers) did not already know. Scripture tells us that some were granted the gift of interpretation of tongues also along with many other supernatural evidences like healings, prophecy, words of knowledge and wisdom.

Evidence that Gentiles were being converted to faith in Christ: Even as Peter was saying these things, the Holy Spirit fell upon all who were listening to the message. The Jewish believers who came with Peter were amazed that the gift of the Holy Spirit had been poured out on the Gentiles, too. (For they heard them speaking in tongues and praising God. (Acts 11:44-46)

The Holy Spirit chose to make His presence noticeable

---

26   John 20:24-29

in Gentiles through the utterance of unknown languages. The Jewish believers needed proof because of the times in which they lived and the newness of this occurrence that God was indeed building His kingdom throughout the world. The time of the Church of Jesus Christ had begun and all the peoples of the world were now coming into the kingdom of God!

Today we are in a similar cultural situation as the early church in that we live among the diverse cultures of the world. Evidence of the reality of Christ is still needed to awaken the lost and the religiously indoctrinated to the fact that God is able to make Himself known. In our day, people still need to know that God has provided a way of connecting with us, not only through the work of Jesus Christ His son, but also by the impartation of His Spirit. The empowerment of Holy Spirit for boldness and utterance is still breaking strongholds of doubt, unbelief and religiosity. In my opinion we need the Pentecost of God more now than ever before!

My Experience of Being Filled

At salvation I invited God to take over the driver's seat of my life which, as I learned to yield and release to Him, happened. This process continues even to this day, as I yield and agree, God does His part to steer and direct me.

As I have told in my journey, I was unaware I could ask Him for deeper experience and in fact for a time was fairly satisfied spiritually with learning the Scriptures and trying to live by them.

Then my life was rocked by the loss of five babies through miscarriages. These very difficult days shook me and brought about a crisis of faith. I questioned God's love and goodness: Was He kind? Did He care not only about how I was hurting, but also about my other children's grief over the losses? As I lived through several years of loss, struggle, and questioning, God was at work. He orchestrated several key events that broke me free from the self-effort, mediocrity and doubt in my Christian life.

First: I was invited to a women's retreat at which

the idea that God could speak personally and directly to me was planted and experienced. God spoke to me through the annoying chirping of a bird as I sat alone on a rock straining to hear His external baritone voice. The annoying little creature kept squeaking away...then I heard an inner voice... "This is just like your life Yvonne – your circumstances annoy you, but I am using them to draw you. Stop trying. Stop straining to figure Me out. I am here. I love you. Trust Me." The voice was more like internal thoughts but they sure were not mine and I felt the kindness of God envelop me.

Secondly: I attended a Steps to Freedom course to which I had been invited. The course was very simple and direct: we needed to repent of old practices and allegiances as well as ancestral sin and other spiritual hindrances.

In the weeks that followed, I noted a change within me. I was no longer satisfied with just learning about God or hearing of the wonders He did in Scripture; I wanted to experience Him first hand! I felt the drawing of God.

My longing for God kindled into passionate hunger to know Him, feel Him with me, to hear His voice daily... or I would quit!! Fortunately, without me understanding or knowing it, my renouncing past hindrances at the "Steps" course had indeed lifted the cloud of apathy and doubt that had hung over me. I was now ready to receive the deeper life I had wondered about for so long.

Next: My husband Bob and I went to an outreach event to participate in the worship which was being led by some friends. At the conclusion of the meeting the speaker, Bryce Hughes, invited any who would like prayer to come to the front of the hall. I was one among many who responded and formed a line of people across the front. My particular desire at this point was to pray for my father, who was terminally ill, that he would receive Jesus and have peace with God.

As Bryce prayed along the line of people, I noticed some of them falling over. I had seen this before and had been told it was fake - not God. I thought to myself, "Oops! I'm in the wrong line!" So I decided leave. However, as I turned I found my escape had been blocked by the overhead projector and some chairs that had been pushed behind me (perhaps it was an angel at work!) There was no way out... I had to face my fear of being weird, being pushed or, even worse, that something spiritual was happening!

Bryce placed his hand lightly on my shoulder and prayed for my father. All seemed normal. Next, he prayed for a fresh filling of Holy Spirit for me and I began to feel the sweet and loving presence of God, like a blanket of love and peace had descended upon me. I felt as if I was melting into a warm pleasant pool. It was the most delightful experience and I found myself sitting quite happy, on the floor without really knowing how I got there. One thing was for certain, this was the most wonderful way to receive more of God. I was no longer afraid or in doubt that God could touch me and make Himself physically felt.

In the days and weeks that followed I began to notice changes in my spiritual life. I started to experience some of the gifts of the Spirit like word of knowledge and prophecy. Furthermore, I received a prayer language, that is, the gift of tongues. I also noticed the fruit of the Spirit flowing from me more intensely: I was filled with greater love, joy, and peace. I have noticed that as I ask God to fill me and as I yield to His promptings, this kind of transformation continues: I grow to know and love Him more and more.

Application

We are told in Scripture not to be drunk with wine, but rather to be filled with the Spirit[27]. Indeed, we see this parallel in the account of the disciples being accused of drunkenness when they were overwhelmed by Holy Spirit on the day of Pentecost.

As we think of Holy Spirit infilling in these terms, some things become evident:

- Holy Spirit filling, thought there is an initial time, is not just a one-time occurrence. We are to keep being filled each day.

---

27   Ephesians 5:18

- We must choose to be filled with Him as opposed to filling ourselves with worldly substitutes – these can occupy our souls in place of Holy Spirit.

- Oil and wine at the time of the writing of scripture were understood in their regular, everyday consumption, as well as for special occasions of celebration. God has chosen to use oil and wine as metaphors of His Spirit because just like the daily need and the special occasions He ordains, the Spirit of God is available to empower us for purpose.

- The infilling of Holy Spirit is a noticeable phenomenon, both by observers and by those who are being filled.

Some Evidences of Holy Spirit Infilling

Being filled with the Holy Spirit, we begin to experience and operate in:

The Grace of Holy Spirits nature: His seven-fold spirit is imparted to us as well as our hope, righteousness, truth, life, and the Spirit of prophecy[28]. We can draw from all he is.

The gifts of the Spirit: healing, miracles, supernatural revelation such as words of knowledge, wisdom and prophecy, and the utterance of languages not known to the speaker ("tongues") and interpretation of these languages.

Fruit of the Spirit: love, joy, peace, patience, gentleness, goodness, faith, humility, temperance/ moderation.

By Faith, Receive

Just as you received salvation by faith, so you may receive fresh infilling of Holy Spirit by faith. Upon your conversion, Holy Spirit took up residence within your human spirit;

---

28   See Chapter 2

when you invited Him and confessed your repentance for any wrongdoing and unbelief, He cleansed your spirit. Although you may not be experiencing it to the extent He has planned, you have His presence within so all He has already resides within you: you are a partaker of His nature, which is given to empower you for His work. You can follow the example of Jesus Christ and fulfill God's purpose for you, as well as enjoy full communion with God. All His attributes have come to rest in you.

As you ask for and receive fresh infilling on an ongoing basis, He will take more room within you and empower you to flow in Him: as the Scriptures say, from your belly (inner-man) will flow rivers of living water[29]. Just as it is a command from Scripture to be filled, it is also a choice to present your body as a living sacrifice[30], to wait upon God to fill you with power and to be filled daily. Activate your faith and receive His filling:

- Come to Jesus and ask expectantly to receive His good gift, as per Jesus' counsel in Luke 11:11-13.

- Ask people who have been baptized by Holy Spirit lay hands on you, agreeing with you in prayer for Spirit infilling, as illustrated in Acts 8:17.

- Give voice to the language of praise that bubbles up from within. St Augustine wrote of a phenomenon he called jubilation which we may today call singing in the spirit. And for whom is such jubilation fitting if not for the ineffable God? For He is ineffable whom one cannot express in words; and if you cannot express Him in words, and yet you cannot remain silent either, then what is left but to sing in jubilation, so that your heart may rejoice without words, and your unbounded joy may not be confined by the limits of syllables. This is often how people first express their prayer language- through singing the sounds of worship

29   John 7:38
30   Romans 12:1

without formulating our own words. Express your worship through sounds the Spirit gives you to voice.

Address Your Fear

Sometimes misunderstandings about Holy Spirit's ministry can cause unwarranted fear of losing control, and this can block our ability to receive from God. The remedy for fear is God's perfect love which casts out fear[31]. Simply repent for being afraid to receive from God and ask for His perfect love to fill you.

Unbelief

Holy Spirit is God, just as the Father and the Son are; as such, faith in Him and His work is essential to the activity of God in our lives. If we hold to the idea that Holy Spirit has ceased to operate in the power the Scriptures attribute to Him, we are in unbelief. Nowhere in Scripture are we told that Holy Spirit would cease to give God's people gifts or fruit. He is the power from on high which the disciples first received, and we would be in error to say or expect any less of Him today.

There is teaching that the supernatural gifts of the Spirit are not for today; this teaching dishonours the Spirit of God, it is not validated in Scripture, and it has caused the people of God to lack faith for the amazing miracles and greater things that Jesus said we could and would do[32]. I have personally repented for unbelief in this area, and have chosen to welcome Holy Spirit and all He has to give me. God has abundantly blessed me with His presence and I am now enjoying a much fuller experience of His presence in my life, accompanied by the supernatural grace, gifts and fruit of His Wonderful Spirit.

Those who are not experiencing the biblical fullness of

31   John 4:18
32   John 14:12

the Holy Spirit may, like me, need to repent of limiting beliefs and ask for a fresh immersion of Holy Spirit. Receive power from on high and watch God do wonderful work through you!

Passivity

Many people are hindered from receiving and flowing in Holy Spirit due to misunderstanding of their part and God's part in the activation process (moving in union with the flow of the Spirit). Like a divine dance, both partners must move together with corresponding steps. As Holy Spirit takes the lead, we sense His movement and reciprocate with matching steps.

The scripture commands us to be filled, to keep receiving Gods Spirit so as to actively take in fresh Spirit filling on an ongoing basis[33]. We are to ask, seek and knock all these relate to actively seeking the things of the Spirit[34].

Suggested Meditation or Journaling Exercise
Holy Spirit please speak to me about being filled

---

33 Ephesians 5:18 here be filled speaks of to keep being filled.
34 Matthew 7; 6-13

Chapter 5 – Revealer of Truth

Jesus Christ is the way, the truth, and the life and Scripture tells us He is the only way to the Father. Truth sets us free to follow God, to live from a perspective of love and to walk into our destiny.

Out of love for us, God gave us the life of Christ as our historic example of what it looks like to live from truth and union with the Father. It is so helpful and moving to read and imagine Jesus in His times of intimate communion with the Father and in the relationships with people He loved. We see this union as Jesus taught, served and worked in agreement with the Father's will! Even more wonderful is that Jesus' life was lived as a show and tell to us so that we may be like Him.

One of the first things we note about Jesus was that He spoke to, listened to, and saw His Father in heaven, whilst being here on the planet. This relationship of loving communion between the Father and the Son has been made available to us as well, thanks to Holy Spirit.

How God Speaks to Us

Many of us have learned to discern the unspoken body language of others, which helps us to fully understand the intent behind the spoken words – or to better understand what is communicated when words are not used at all. We can often tell when a friend is upset, depressed, angry, or happy by their body language. By watching how they move or physically respond; as we engage with them, we see and hear their communication.

In fact, we communicate in many ways when we are at a distance from others, whether by Email, FaceBook, Twitter, greeting cards, or giving gifts. We can be quite creative in communicating, so how much more is the Creator creative in how He can communicate with us!

God is continuously speaking messages of love, encouragement, comfort, wisdom, correction, direction, and more. He wants to help and guide us so that we receive all the benefit of His great wisdom and care. He does not want us to be without direction and lost but rather to be accompanied by Him throughout life, not missing any good thing He has planned for us.

Each of us has a native or first language with which we learned to communicate, that of our parents or caregivers. In a similar way we have at least one avenue or language through which we receive revelation from God. This chapter is a brief overview of the ways God communicates to us through the languages He speaks.

While most Christians recognize the Bible as their primary way to hear God, most of us also have other languages such as those explained below. We can, if we choose, learn to hear God through all of these.

Often God speaks through the mysteries or puzzles of: life's circumstances, nature, our senses, our emotions, dreams, music, and even the current world events through media. These messages are at times not clear to us at first. They are in fact starting points of the conversation that God is initiating, like an opening or one-liner with which a conversation begins.

For example, we may see a strange natural occurrence, notice a road sign or newspaper headline; we may hear a song on the radio. We can recognize these everyday occurrences as opportunities for God to speak on a topic we are pondering. The Holy Spirit will inwardly say, "Look at that, now that's something you don't see every day!" God is opening a topic for you to interact with Him about. God loves us and wants to dialogue with us, so take the hint - LISTEN, chat it over with Him, and ponder what the Lord is saying to you.

As you read this chapter, I encourage you to find your first language in God. Ask Him to expand your experience of Him in hearing His voice through the many languages He speaks.

Hearing God Through Scripture

The Bible or Scripture is for most Christians the primary way to receive revelation or hear from God. Through meditative reading (slow, thoughtful, repetitive reading), we often sense God's voice pointing to particular words, verses, and passages from Scripture which relate to our current situation or need. Often people perceive a passage highlighted to them by the Holy Spirit's prompting from within.

We know from 2 Timothy 3:16 that all Scripture is God-breathed.

The Scriptures themselves are the Logos or written word, and the Holy Spirit-highlighted passage is the Rhema or personal revelation/ word to the individual[35]. Not only is the Bible our means for receiving revelation from God, it is an essential tool for testing all revelation as to whether it is from God, our own thoughts, or of evil/ negative source.

Because Scripture reveals the nature and character of God, we can discern if the message we are receiving is in alignment with Him according to whether it is in agreement with His written word. Indeed, revelation, however it comes, must be in agreement with the principles set out in the Scriptures. (See Testing Revelation, Chapter 7 for more on this.)

---

35   A further distinction between the two Greek terms Rhema and Logos can help us grasp two aspects of God's "word":

Rhema, at times called "spoken word," refers to the revelation received by us when Holy Spirit speaks to our hearts, as referred to in John 14:17,26.

Logos refers to the Word of God, the person of Christ, the Bible from Genesis to Revelation.

Our Circumstances

God will often get our attention through unusual or troubling circumstances in order to cause us to stop and ask for direction. Sometimes we have become too distracted to hear Him, and God will allow change that will cause us to slow down so that we will enquire of Him and wait for His answer.

Negative things like a financial need can cause us to come to Him for guidance; job loss, sickness, relational difficulties may draw us to Him for wisdom and help. Blessings also carry the potential for us to come to God; for example, the prospect of becoming a parent, a new job, a financial windfall, a location change could remind us of our need for wisdom and bring us to seek God for it. He can use a shift in our circumstances to refocus our lives and to move us into our destiny.

Natural Surroundings

God will speak to us through the world around us and the people we interact with every day, especially if we have asked Him a question or are asking for wisdom and direction. Our part in hearing Him is to be open and aware that the One who created and loves us wants to guide us and answer our questions. Often the voice of God comes to us as we go about life, doing everyday activities. Holy Spirit is the one who alerts us to notice when God is using our circumstances, natural surroundings, or the words of other people.

God has spoken to me through weather changes, earthquakes, trees, flowers, insects, animal and human behaviour, along with signs on buildings and vehicles. He is so very creative in the way He communicates!

I have been given wisdom through animals and birds when Holy Spirit has quickened me to notice a different behaviour or something unusual. For example, a pair of raccoons once came to a very spindly tree in my yard in the country and perched in a branch in broad daylight. There was very little foliage to hide them and when our family took notice, the animals just kept very still and "played possum" as we say in Australia, meaning they pretended to be asleep or dead.

The occurrence was so unusual I felt God was speaking through it. As I later prayed and pondered the raccoon couple's odd behaviour I realized God was giving me insight into the character of a young couple our family had been assisting.

Raccoons are masked and these were trying to deceive us into thinking they were just sleeping, not up to anything like getting into the garbage and making a mess. The young couple too were pretending and had the potential of causing a big mess for us if we allowed them the opportunity. We were able to help them from a distance and avoid the mess they could have created for us because of their love of "garbage" which translated into a love for sin.

An amazing incident my husband Bob witnessed serves as another example of God speaking through what is "un-naturally" natural. He was taking a lunch break in the parking lot of the company for which he had been contracted to work when he saw something fall from the sky and hit the shiny new blue truck of one of the co-workers. The co-worker had just lovingly polished and parked his new truck away from the other vehicles in order that it would be safe from any accidents or dust.

The object fell from seemingly nowhere and hit the truck with such force it bent the antenna backward and slid across the parking lot sliding to a stop some distance away. Other men on their break heard the impact but only Bob saw the object which as they examined noted to be a fish, specifically a carp. Bob took pictures of the gasping fish and called the unbelieving owner of the truck to see the cause of the bent antenna and bloodied mess on the hood of his beloved truck.

At the time of the impact Bob had been pondering what he was doing working in this particular place. God's message to him was provision and evangelism, both of which are linked for Bob who loves to evangelize in his workplace. God was confirming and encouraging Bob in his calling; also, perhaps the man who owned the truck needs to get his antenna up as it seems God is getting his attention!

People
Many of us have listened to a sermon and have realized God was using the words of the speaker to communicate His personal message to us. Interestingly, however, God can and regularly does speak through regular, everyday people who cross our paths; after all, the Scriptures say that God is not a respecter of persons, meaning no matter their social position or status God sees all people of equal value. This is very much the case when He is communicating with us: God will speak through the mouth of a homeless person or millionaire with equal significance to our lives; the interpreter is Holy Spirit who quickens us to realize it was a word from God.

I have had prophetic messages through songs on the radio, cashiers, ministers, prophets and children. All were significant and were indeed God's voice to me, even though many of these people did not know they were speaking on behalf of God; indeed, some would have been shocked at the thought! Nonetheless, God used what they said to speak me.

Dreams
Dreams are like a detective story, where the dreamer receives a number of clues which need to be pieced together to formulate a message – the end result may be quite different than what would have appeared to be communicated on the surface. As dreams are often symbolic and can arise from God, your own mind and emotions, or from the enemy, it is important to pray over your sleep hours just as you would over your days.

Many people have blockages to their dream life because of unbelief, fear of nightmares, or because they have spoken curses over their ability to dream ("I don't dream", "I never remember my dreams", etc.). If this is the case, repentance and asking for cleansing of the imagination's capacity is a good restorative measure. In the case of nightmares, it could be that there is an opening for the enemy due to a polluting of the imagination (for example: watching horror movies, explicit and violent visual material, etc.); this too can be repented of, and our dream life rededicated with prayer, each night before sleep.

We receive messages from God through dreams because we take time to explore and enquire for the answer. After all, God wants us to draw near to Him and talk with Him about our lives; He is very relational and will stir us to come to Him through this mysterious communication[36].

Emotion

God can use our emotions to speak to us about our own needs, the needs of others, and the spiritual atmosphere in our surroundings. Emotions can also show how He feels about a situation or person.

Holy Spirit has often given me the emotions of a person I am praying for so I can intercede with passion, knowing their feelings. I have also felt the emotion-charged atmosphere when I have come into a place where prayer is needed. For example, whilst prayer-walking a neighbourhood, I could tangibly feel the change in atmosphere when we crossed over a street to a low-income housing project. I felt the hopelessness, depression, and anger of the residents and so I prayed for God's help and provision as well as His love, peace, and joy to prevail there.

Many times when I have been involved in prayer ministry with individuals, I have felt God's heart or emotions for them. I have in fact been overwhelmed with His great loving-kindness, His delight over them as well as His sadness over their brokenness. This emotional burden-bearing for God is a wonderful gift for us as we intercede for others.

In hearing God through emotions we need to use discernment by asking God from whom or where this emotion is coming; He will give us understanding as to the source of the feeling and what to do with it. If you sense unrest or negative emotions in an environment or person,

---

36   For more information on dreams or vision see The Language of Dreams and Visions by Rev. Yvonne Prentice (Ottawa: August 2013), available from the author.

very often the Lord wants us to take authority and release His power supernaturally. We may be led to release the opposite emotion or spirit in prayer; if we sense fear, for example, we release perfect love.

As we agree with God's leading and pray according to it we will see real change and help come to people and places we are sent to by the grace of the Holy Spirit. It is truly a wondrous thing that God would share His heart with us so we may partner with Him in kingdom work.

Inner Knowing

Many people – often creative thinkers or right-brain dominant – are led by Holy Spirit in a very natural inward way. Called inner knowing, this awareness or sense of God's desires and thoughts operates much like a word of knowledge[37]. The person receives Spirit-to-spirit revelation and just knows what the Lord is saying.

This experience is the way most revelation comes to us. We are quickened by the Holy Spirit as He communes with our spirit and reveals God's thoughts and understanding to us. Revelation from this deep Spirit-to-spirit communion bubbles up into our senses so that our brain can process what God is communicating.

We will often miss the inner knowing if we are not aware that this intuition or knowing is from God: We can second-guess the message, thinking it is just human intuition. We need to pay attention, as with the other senses, and ask Holy Spirit if it is His thought or revelation, then act accordingly. We cannot assume that every thought we have is a "God thought" but we can be assured that some will be; as we agree with God and use discernment, more and more of our thoughts will be aligned with His.

We grow in discernment as we draw near and listen to His Spirit daily, and become accustomed to the inner voice of God.

---

37   See 1 Corinthians 12:8.

Our Spiritual Senses

From childhood we have learned to experience the natural world through our five senses: sight, sound, taste, touch, smell. God has likewise given us senses within our spirit with which we can experience Him and the spiritual world. The senses of spiritual seeing and hearing are excellent tools for communing with God.

For many people, either hearing God's voice through words/thoughts in their minds or seeing divine pictures/visions are functional and growing avenues of connecting with Him from an early age. We could call these capacities their first language as far as communion with God is concerned. As with natural language, if hearing or vision is not our first language, we can nonetheless learn these languages or tools to expand our ability to understand God's communication. We can recognize the importance of seeing (spiritual vision) and hearing God's voice as important methods because Jesus our Lord exemplified their use[38].

Seeing

Not only are we commanded to fix our eyes upon Jesus and to follow His example of looking to see what His Father was doing, we are also told some of the benefits of spiritual vision:

- that the eyes of your heart may be flooded with light (Ephesians 1:18) so we can understand the confident hope that is our inheritance;

- that your eyes may always be on the Lord for He rescues you from the traps of your enemies (Psalm 25:15);

- to reveal or prophesy of things to come (Revelation 1:1); and

- to impassion you to run your race with endurance, stripping off any entanglements of sin. (Hebrews 12:1-2)

---

38   See John 5:19-20.

- Furthermore, spiritual vision is the reward for the pure in heart (Matthew 5:8), and

- revelations bring understanding and instruction. (2 Corinthians 12:1-7)

I too have found that using the eyes of my heart to see is very valuable in hearing the voice of God through my internal sense of "hearing". Each morning as I spend time with Jesus, I ask Holy Spirit to show me where Jesus is with me. I will sense Christ to be with me; as I begin to see with my inner eye where He is, the way I see Him also shows me what He wants to talk about. For example, when Holy Spirit directs me to see Jesus in my kitchen, Jesus often speaks to me about the Scriptures; this either teaches me a new concept that I may teach others, or some fresh truth to edify, correct, or train me in righteousness. After all, the Scriptures are spiritual food that strengthen my life!

Another example of how seeing Jesus enables me to hear from God is by focusing, looking to Jesus when I pray for others. I see Jesus show me how to pray or show me something that will help them to understand His work in their lives[39].

Activation

If we are not natural seers (those for whom picturing is the way they receive from God), we can learn to see vision. We can "oil the wheels" or "prime the pump" of vision by opening our inner eyes (eyes of our hearts) and picturing with our imagination what the Lord will show us.

Following are steps that may be necessary to overcoming obstacles to seeing vision and dreaming God-given dreams.

- We need to repent for unbelief and for cursing our vision with words like "I can't" or "I never dream or see visions".

- We may need to repent of looking at images (e.g.

---

39   See "Praying like Jesus", Chapter 8.

horror movies, sexually explicit pictures) that have damaged or marred our imaginations.

- To open our spiritual vision we need to know it is biblical to look, as shown in Revelation 1:10-12 and 4:1-2. Remember, Jesus looked into the spiritual realm (in heaven) to see what His Father was doing, then did on earth what He saw.

- Exercise your spiritual vision and cleanse it by meditating and picturing passages of Scripture like Psalms 1, 23, and 91[40] as well as any for the visions of the prophets[41] and the scenes from the gospels where Jesus was ministering[42].

- We need to dedicate our imaginations and spiritual vision to God. You may want to use the following prayers or pray in your own words.

Prayer of Repentance
"Lord Jesus, I repent for using my imagination to dwell on, the eyes of my heart to see, and my ears to hear ungodly things. I ask You to forgive me for anything I have taken into my eyes, ears, and imagination that has been sinful or offensive to You. I forgive myself for seeing, hearing, or imagining sinful material. I receive Your forgiveness. Amen."

Dedication Prayer:
"Thank You Lord Jesus for Your example of doing what You saw Your Father do. I purpose by Your power now to use the eyes of my heart, my imagination to honour You. I dedicate

---

40   Focus on a vivid illustration like the trees and chaff in Psalm 1; picture the Shepherd with Whom you walk, as described in Psalm 23; with the eyes of your heart, see Psalm 91's images of the shelter found in the promise of the Most High.
41   Imagine partaking in the experience of a prophet's vision, such as that in Ezekiel 1.
42   Place yourself in one of the Gospel accounts of Jesus' ministry: imagine being a bystander in Luke 5:11 or a witness of Matthew 8:14-15.

to You my imagination and my visual capacities and all of my senses; thank You for the dreams You give to educate me in the night. I give You permission to activate my senses, to use my imagination and to give me dreams. Amen."

Hearing

John 10:27 tells us that God's sheep hear His voice, He knows them, they follow Him, and nothing can pluck them out of His hand. For some, hearing God's voice happens easily and spontaneously and they naturally learn to recognize the still, small voice: hearing God through words or thoughts is their first language. For many others, hearing and discerning the voice of God must be learned and practiced; as the Scriptures teach, God's sheep can and do hear His voice so we can be assured it is God's will to listen for His voice.

While at times God will interrupt our daily activities to speak in a particular moment, it is also wonderful to hear from Him continually, throughout the day because we choose to tune in to His still small voice, as described in 1 Kings 19:11-13. We stay connected to our Father in this way, known as practicing the presence of Christ, or referred to as praying without ceasing (something that would be impossible to do if we were the ones doing all the talking!)

Through the 1 Kings Scripture, we discover what God's voice sounds like most of the time, a "still small voice" or, put another way, spontaneous thoughts that gently come into our minds. That is, God's voice sounds like our thoughts but they are much wiser, more loving, and kinder than our thoughts. They are "thoughts" we have not been thinking and do not involve the intentional use of our own cognitive reasoning: God speaks through our minds but not from our minds. He communes Spirit to spirit and His communication bubbles up from our spirit into our minds as thoughts, so that we can hear His voice, respond to Him, and know Him.

In this book I have provided exercises in the form of questions which will help you to tune in to God's voice. You may also use questions to help with focusing your inner ears to hear God as you commune with Him daily. For example, each morning I begin my day by asking God what He would like to say to me in the course of that day. Then I quiet myself, picture Jesus, and tune in to the inner thoughts and words that begin to flow. I write down what I have sensed God say, then when I am finished listening and writing, I discern and judge if I have heard God by comparing it to God's character, His principles given in the Bible.

Hearing God through journaling His voice is a subject larger than we can address in this book but I pray you are helped by this brief teaching. You, can and probably already do hear His voice.

A wonderful example of hearing God through His still small voice is that of Johannes Brenz a Lutheran reformer, who was warned by an "inner voice" of the approach of the Spanish army at Stuttart. The inner voice instructed him to go to a certain building in the upper city, find an open door, enter it and hide under the roof. He obeyed, found the door and hid as the voice had instructed. His hiding place was visited by a hen that daily laid two eggs for him until the danger was past. How wonderful it is to hear Gods voice and experience his amazing love, provision, and protection.

Another way God can speak to us through our auditory sense is by music; many hear God through this language, not only through the words of a song but also through the sound of the music, beat, rhythm, and melody. In fact I have had several clear words from God through the songs of birds!

Simple Steps Towards Hearing God's Voice

We may need to "oil the wheels" or "prime the pump" of our inner ears by asking a question, just as picturing opens our inner eyes; stilling ourselves before God allows us to listen. If we accompany these steps to hearing God with picturing we will find it much easier to discern His voice. As we hear His thoughts, it is advisable to write down what we hear so we can read and test what we are hearing after with Scripture and the character of God. You may follow these steps to enable you to hear God's voice.

Repent of any negative words. Pray a simple prayer to renounce any negative words that may have hindered you from hearing God. Forgive anyone for word curses they have said over you. Receive your forgiveness for sin that may be disturbing your ability to come to God. Repent for wrong use of your hearing (listening to negative or blasphemous words or music). Dedicate your inner ears to God.

Become still. Find a quiet place and come into stillness within by focusing on Jesus Christ. You may wish to whisper His name gently and slowly to settle inwardly.

Picture Jesus. You may ask Holy Spirit where Jesus is in the room with you or picture yourself in a comfortable scene with Him.

Ask a simple, open question. "How do You see me, God?" and "What do You want to say to me about hearing Your voice, seeing You, being with You?" are good starting points. I make it my practice to begin my day with the question "What do You want to say to me today, Lord?"

Keep your question simple and open-ended so that you will not be receiving a yes or no answer. God desires to spend time with you and commune with you. Yes or no answers shorten the conversation; the Lord wants relationship which requires you getting to know His heart for you.

Record your conversation. It is good to keep a journal of your dreams, visions, and God's words to you. Date each conversation or revelatory experience so you can re-read and test them at a later date.

Test what you have heard. When we are learning a new skill, we often benefit from mentors and the advice of more experienced friends. It is a wonderful encouragement and support to have several trusted friends who can help you to discern if you are on track and hearing God.

You can always ask God to give you confirmation on what you are unsure of. I have often been given Scripture verses which, when I then found them in the word, confirmed what God had been speaking to me in my time of listening[43].

---

43   See "Testing Revelation", Chapter 7.

Taste, Touch, and Smell

God's language can arise through all of our senses and often grows as we spend more time listening and waiting on the Lord; like any love relationship, it flourishes the more we give ourselves to it. Holy Spirit will at times expand our language through the use of taste, touch, and smell. These senses can activate individually or come as a multi-sensory experience where vision and hearing may be involved.

We have found that senses may be used as confirmation of something God has been speaking previously; on their own, they often need interpretation. The fragrance of the Lord for example has brought me and many others into the awareness of God's presence with them in there quiet times with Him as well as occasions when assurance of His nearness is needed. Another example of the sense of smell is the experience I had of smelling scent of oranges, which meant to me sweet fruitfulness of God was active.

A touch on the hand could be interpreted as God speaking about direction[44].

The taste of honey can represent the sweet presence of God. As scripture alludes Jesus Christ is sweeter than honey. Once again testing revelation of this kind is essential.

Suggested Meditation or Journaling Exercise

Lord, speak to me about how I can grow in hearing Your voice.

---

[44]   Covered in detail in "The Language of Dreams and Visions" under the Dictionary of Symbols - Body Parts.

Chapter 6 – Spiritual Disciplines

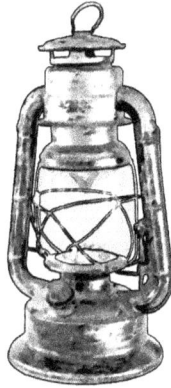

Also called spiritual practices or, spiritual disciplines are actions and activities regularly used to move us along a path toward spiritual growth, closer union with God, and the personal spiritual freedom. Listening prayer, meditation, fasting, and intentional times of intimacy with God as well as the incorporation of; silence, solitude, singing and worship are all considered spiritual disciplines that strengthen and give vitality to the life of faith and friendship with God.

Listening Prayer

The terms *listening prayer, stillness, waiting on the Lord,* and *soaking* in God's presence are terms for very similar practices within the realm of intentional times of spiritual intimacy. Becoming still or being quiet inwardly allows us to focus on God and hear Him. Soaking in God's presence is the current term for stillness for an extended period (usually one or two hours). Being still before God was practiced by the ancients and has many references in Scripture:

Psalm 2:1-3 The Lord is my shepherd; I shall not want. He makes me to lie down in green pastures; He leads me beside the still waters. He restores my soul...

Psalm 27:14 Wait on the Lord; be of good courage and He shall strengthen your heart. Wait I say, on the Lord!

Psalm 37:7 Rest in the Lord and wait patiently for

Him.

Psalm 131:2 Surely I have calmed and quieted my soul, like a weaned child and his mother; like a weaned child is my soul within me.

Proverbs 1:33 But whoever listens to Me will dwell safely, and will be secure without fear of evil.

Isaiah 40:29 He gives power to the weak, and to those who have no might He increases strength. Even the youths shall faint and be weary, and the young men shall utterly fall, but those who wait on the Lord shall renew their strength. They shall mount up with wings like eagles. They shall run and not be weary; they shall walk and not faint.

Hosea 2:14 Therefore, behold, I will allure her. I will bring her into the wilderness and speak comfort to her.

Matthew 11:28-30 Come to Me, all you who labour and are heavy laden, and I will give you rest. Take My yoke upon you and learn from Me, for I am gentle and lowly in heart, and you will find rest for your souls. For My yoke is easy and my burden is light.

Luke 10:39 And she had a sister called Mary, who sat at Jesus' feet and heard His word.

Hebrews 4:9-11 There remains therefore a rest for the people of God. For who has entered His rest has himself also ceased from his works as God did from His. Let us therefore be diligent to enter that rest.

We see soaking or listening prayer with music in the presence of the Lord modeled by Elisha the prophet in 2 Kings 3:15-16: 'Now bring me someone who can play the harp'. While the harp was being played, the power of the Lord came upon Elisha, and he said, 'This is what the Lord says.'

David the Psalmist too knew the value and delight of resting in God's presence with an attitude of worship. In 1 Samuel 16:14-22, David "soaked" King Saul with music to bring him into peace and stillness. Like many of us, David was not a perfect person, yet he pleased God, Who called him a man after His own heart.

Levels of Stillness

Becoming still is the process of quieting the inner being. To accomplish inner quiet we often need to settle outer distractions and then to focus inwardly. We move our attention inward; from the outer body to quieting the soul (mind, will, emotions, imagination and conscience) so as to commune with the Holy Spirit Who indwells our human spirit.

In order for us to enjoy communion with God, to hear His voice through tuning inward to Holy Spirit, we need to hush the noise around us and within us. Following are some simple steps that may assist you as you learn to become still and hear God.

Allow time. As you learn to relax and meet with God you will need to dedicate some time to the process. Time constraint can cause unrest. Clock watching is a distraction which can be removed by setting a timer. Give yourself 10 to 15 minutes to settle into awareness.

Remove outer distractions. It is best at first to be alone, as electronic devices, phone calls, the movement of other people and pets will cause interruptions. Gather things you may need: pen, notepad, glass of water and perhaps a blanket for warmth.

Make yourself physically comfortable, since issues with body comfort can cause restlessness. For you rest could be a position of lying down, sitting, standing or walking. While each body knows which position suits it best, choose one that is different from your normal sleep posture (if lying down is what's most comfortable). For those who feel most relaxed while walking, choose a quiet, solitary place to stroll.

Remove inner distractions. Relax; put a little smile on your lips. You may want to whisper the name of Jesus several times to focus your thoughts. Perhaps you will not need any further steps before you begin to sense God.

For some, however, this is when the mind begins to flit about or go into activity. Don't try to force the quieting of the mind, just listen to the thoughts and see what the issue is. If you need to address distractions of the mind, ask Holy Spirit,

"What are my thoughts?" Listen to the thoughts that flow from the question. He will reveal any area of concern.

Listed below are common concerns and how to quieten them:

- For worry: Give the concern over to God in prayer. Tell Him you trust Him to hold the issue (or person) for your time together. Picture the concern in God's hands and command worry to be silent in the name of Jesus.

- For the to-do list: Simply write the list down and allow your mind the peace of knowing you will not forget but will get to the list later.

- People for whom you may pray: Even the needs of others must be put on hold for the time being. Just make a note of the names and purpose to pray for them. This is your time to personally connect and hear God's heart for you.

- Sin consciousness: Awareness of sin and our own inadequacies can be a barrier to meeting with God. God has provided very excellent help for us in that Jesus has more than paid for our debt with His sinless life poured out on the cross. Just bring yourself to Him afresh and agree with Him for your cleansing and restoration. Receive your forgiveness. Allow Him to wash over you in loving acceptance and move into communion with Him unhindered.

Remember that condemnation, guilt, and shame are not sent from God. He takes you as you are. By His precious blood, you are now fully accepted into His family as a son and heir. Your inheritance is now to fully enjoy your Father, and allow Him to fully enjoy communion with you.

Dedication Prayer

You may want to use the following prayer or pray in your own words.

"Thank You for Your love and acceptance of me as Your child. I dedicate this time to be with You. Lord, I am listening - I am Yours and You are my God. The voice of a stranger and the voice of the enemy I will not hear. Thank You that I have the mind of Christ. I give You permission now, Holy Spirit, to supersede my thinking and speak to me through all of my faculties. I open myself up to You - Father, Son, and Holy Spirit. Amen."

Worship and Attune

Gratitude and worship (admiration for God and His ways) are the doorway into communion. Allow your mind to settle into thoughts of God, His attributes, His love and kindness toward you. Tell Him inwardly how you feel about Him. Whisper His name and inwardly welcome His presence. Tune in to flowing thoughts, pictures, and feelings. Relax and receive.

You may now transition into soaking or listening prayer.

Suggested Meditation or Journaling Exercise

Holy Spirit, what is the importance of becoming still?

Holy Spirit, speak to me about hearing You through an avenue I have not yet experienced.

Meditation

Entering into the Mysteries of God

Meditation is the ancient practice of exercising the mind in contemplation[45]. Christian meditation's goal is to slow down to connect with God. Meditation focuses our mind and senses bringing us to an attentive state so that we may digest truth, and realign to God's perspective. As we offer God a dedicated, focused gift of time, the Holy Spirit brings us into alignment, adjusting our inner stance toward God's way of thinking.

---

45   Canadian Oxford Dictionary

The Spirit of God brings us into agreement with the mind of Christ, which is alive within every believer in Jesus Christ. Our minds and hearts need to adjust daily toward our greater purpose. The by-product of this reconnected relationship and purpose is inner peace.

Christian meditation is an active process of the soul (mind, will, emotions, imagination, and conscience). Unlike Eastern religious meditative practices, it is not emptying the soul of thought and overcoming physical distractions, but filling, refuelling, and communing with God our Creator. This inner process of meeting with and "hearing" God allows God's thoughts to reorder our thoughts. Through this we recognize where adjustments need to be made. Meditation gives God the Spirit freedom to move truth and revelation to a deeper level within us so that truth seeds and activates change within us. Our minds are renewed by the activation of truth as God moves through our soul, enlightening, convincing, and convicting us.

Taking in the truths of God is more effective when all of the faculties of the soul are involved through meditation. The focused but relaxed approach of meditation activates all of the souls faculties: whereas the work and exercise of study only involves the mind through human reasoning.

The process of Christian meditation, on Scripture for example, is similar to the activity of memorization with the added benefit of inviting the flow of Holy Spirit into the process. Not to merely get the words exact in the mind, then to use human reasoning to think about the meaning, but to including Holy Spirit's interjection, explanation, and expansion of our understanding . Meditation invites Him to interact with our senses, bringing the scripture or topic alive, through Spirit to spirit revelation internally teaching us. Our stilled and quieted soul is enabled to digest truth as we give God time and focused attention. In order to truly take in spiritual food we must cease from our human striving and let our inner man feed or drink in the things God wants to teach us.

A helpful picture of this process is to view the

difference between our normal process of thinking and learning with the contrasting picture of the meditative process of pondering truth. For example: When we use our reasoning abilities to think through a scripture we begin at point A, which examines the whole passage or verse then, through a process of study (perhaps researching with concordance or Greek/ Hebrew dictionary), we break down the information within the passage and decide what it is telling us. B may be some insight which will cause us to research other things C. that will lead us to D, E and so on till we reach our conclusion at Z. This way of examining the scripture, studying it, is rather like a straight line (Linear thinking) as below.

A • B • C ••• Z

The meditative process looks quite different. We begin at the same point (A) examining the passage or verse but instead of only using the reasoned approach, studying and researching, we apply what I call circular thinking. Meditation employs the brain but does not work at reasoning as with studying. The brain is occupied by repeatedly lifting scripture into the consciousness and receiving the thoughts and impressions from Holy Spirit. The Spirit of God overlays the fragments of scripture with deepening meaning allowing the brain and soul to process each nugget of revelation and internalize them. As we begin reading or replaying the passage several times in its entirety at first then following the Spirit, the brain gradually narrows down our focus to fewer and fewer words or fragments of scripture. A picture of this process would look like concentric circles.

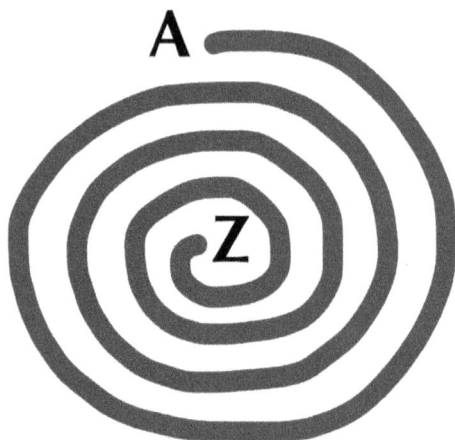

The smaller and smaller concentric circles represent fewer words repeated; in the simplicity of less, comes the beauty of the Holy revelation ever deepening in the soul and spirit. This is the meditative process of spiritual digestion: The truth becoming part of our inner-man.

As with study, the meditative process can take us several sessions to unwrap a passage, depending upon how long a passage we are choosing to ponder. It is best to start with just one thought or verse at a time. If we do choose larger passages be prepared to take several sessions to complete our meditation.

Simple Steps for Biblical Meditation
Become still: quieting yourself is a process of first removing, as much as possible, any outer distractions such as

- Time constraints; set a time to avoid clock watching.

- Prep people who may need your attention as to how long you need solitude, so they will be at peace.

- Telephone and electronic devices need to be off.

- Be physically comfortable so pain or discomfort does not demand your attention. You do not have be physically still if it is painful for you, our aim is inward stillness.

Then move your attention from the outer body to quieting the soul (mind, will, and emotions) so as to commune with the Holy Spirit[46]. Perhaps you will not need any further steps before you begin to sense God. I have found if we employ the mind in meditating on Scripture, and the imagination through pondering, that the emotions and will usually come along for the ride. The conscience may be pricked by a sin consciousness which will be quelled by the cleansing of confession. Following are some practices which take us to inward focus:

- Calling on the name of Jesus: If we call on the name of Jesus He will answer and meet with us. You may want to whisper the name of Jesus several times to focus your thoughts. You may pray the simple Jesus prayer which many people through the ages have prayed to focus their attention: "Lord Jesus Christ have mercy upon me." This prayer is softly and slowly spoken (or thought) till the soul senses the sweet presence of Christ.

- Picturing Jesus: I often picture Him with me by asking the Holy Spirit where Jesus is with me. When I sense where Jesus is I then focus my attention on Him thanking and worshiping Him.

- Connecting with Holy Spirit: I turn my attention to Holy Spirit by offering praise and thanks to him for his presence life and light within me. I focus upon His light within me, giving Him permission to move upon all of my thoughts, senses and emotions. I wait upon Him and then lift up the passage or verse of scripture and begin to ponder in the circular fashion I have described.

- The safety of Father: Often Holy Spirit has prompted me to meet with my Heavenly Father in the safety of His arms. My earthly father was a very safe person for me so it is comforting and helpful as I picture being embraced and loved to ponder truths about His greatness.

If you have a preselected topic or Scripture for meditation, gently turn your thoughts to it. If not, ask God what He would like to give you today. Record your starting point (scripture, topic, question or thought). Begin to ponder by applying circular thinking (the words repeated slowly over and over in the mind) pause between each repetition, rest in each repetition, linger, ponder, allowing time for God's interaction within each repetition.

Continue on the one thought or line of scripture till you sense a deepening of understanding. This may come in the form of[47]:

- Vision: by way of mental pictures or inward videos.

- Thoughts: interjected, spontaneous thoughts. These thoughts are not your thoughts but are much wiser and enlightening.

- Flowing emotions: that give a sense of how Father feels.

- Taste Touch and Smell: God created all of our senses and so He may use them to communicate and deepen our understanding as He leads us into all truth through meditation.

Remember without faith it is impossible to please God and we must come to God believing that He loves us and desires even more than we do to communicate and teach us. We are told in the Scripture to Meditate on His word day and night so our time is well spent and faith well invested as we allow Holy Spirit to deepen us in through the process.

---

47   See "How God speaks", Chapter 5.

Journaling

Record what is coming through words, thoughts, vision, or other senses. As we receive with thankfulness more will be given. Writing down or recording what is happening allows us the freedom to keep receiving knowing we will be able to test and pray over the concepts and thoughts later. Feel free to ask God what He is saying or showing as it is happening. Interact with Him like you do with a close friend, after all He already knows what you are thinking. As you give voice to your own thoughts you are more able to process the communication flowing between you and God. Your clear questions will be met with His clear response and will give your mind a focal point for deeper meditation.

Conclusion

Worship and give thanks for the time together with God. Honour your heavenly Father for the revelation and time He shared with you. It is always good to go over your previous time of meditation before the next time so that you are in flow as you approach Him for the next conversation.

Through this simple process, I have found deeper understanding of God's eternal biblical truth which has enriched my personal walk of faith with Jesus. Before I understood the process of meditation I had a more limited understanding of the scriptures, even though I had read, and memorized them for many years. Through the practice of meditation my love for God and His written word increased along with understanding His wisdom and counsel for every-day decisions. The Logos has in this way become personal revelation (Rhema)[48]. It has quickened my soul thus becoming part of who I am as well as aligning my life in practical ways to Gods truth and will.

God is a wonderful communicator. His desire to commune is greater than ours and He is very good at removing our barriers. In fact Holy Spirit once reassured me in a time of self-doubt that God can speak louder than I

---

48   See "Hearing God Through Scripture", Chapter 5.

can listen so I need not worry that I will be hard of hearing. Our faith is key, but God is in the business of increasing our little faith. After all, faith comes by hearing, and hearing by the word of God. God will increase our faith to receive as we lean on Him to bring us into the depths of friendship. He will reawaken the Garden of Eden within each of us as we take time to be with Him in the cool of the day (the simplicity of quiet moments), just as Adam and Eve once did.

Suggested Meditation or Journaling Exercise

Choose a well-known Scripture, for example Psalm 23, and enter into a time of listening prayer or meditation. Spend time on each phrase and go only as far along into the passage as you feel Holy Spirit giving grace to your understanding. You may find that in one hour you will only be able to ponder 5 verses. Don't rush the process. Enjoy the treasures of wisdom and understanding being revealed. Use the following pages to note the insights you receive.

Choose a topic about which you are concerned - take time to meditate and listen to God's perspective.

Write the insights you are given.

Suggested Meditation or Journaling Exercise

Choose a relationship for which you need insight and ask God about His perspective. Write the insights you receive. NOTE: This is for your understanding only (i.e. not to be used as a letter of correction for the other person(s) involved).

Fasting

The spiritual discipline of fasting has been practiced for centuries and so many differing opinions exist. My personal experience with fasting is certainly not as extensive as some, however, I feel to share some insights I have gained.

The title of fasting given to this practice of denying one's-self in order to draw closer to God is, I feel, is almost opposite to what we do in practice to connect with Him. "Slowing" may be a more accurate descriptive name than "fasting". When we stop normal activities and turn our attention toward God, thus slowing down, we remove distractions, hindrances and even normal activities in favour of focusing on Him.

The Purpose of Fasting

Fasting or abstaining from some daily need awakens our soul toward God. It draws our attention away from our own needs toward our greater need of Him. The purpose of fasting is not to invoke God's attention or presence; since our Father God does not have a problem with focus or connecting with us, we do not need to fast in order to get His attention! Nor is fasting to be taken on for the purpose of making our case more urgent to Him, or to cause Him to change a circumstance or take action on our behalf. If we fast to get something from God, we are actually trying to manipulate Him.

The Benefits of Fasting

Fasting brings focus to life. When we fast, we give undivided attention to God so that we become keenly aware of His presence. We set aside normal, even very much needed requirements (e.g. food, drink/, interaction with others) and less urgent needs (e.g. our use of the telephone, computer, leisure time, exposure to media, or entertainment) to be in communion with Jesus. Communion or time spent in God's presence brings His divine outlook into focus. We are then able to go back to normal life with better perspective and motivation because we have been aligned to God's plan. Even though our circumstances may not change, we come to them with renewed hope and many times a fresh strategy.

Fasting can bring death to our flesh or human, earthly outlook and habits; this in turn enables us to live according to the Holy Spirit's direction. This is because our motivation is to allow God to work the submission (or "death") process within us as we yield to His ways (or "life"). We must be careful, however, to keep in mind the potential for defeating the very purpose of fasting: our flawed human nature can lead down the path of religious pride.

A Word of Caution

Jesus encountered a religious pride in the leaders of His day which seemed to be particularly connected to their practice of regular scheduled fasting. It seems there exists a strong temptation to pride and religious superiority if our choice to fast comes from human decision and not by Holy Spirit's express direction.

I have to confess I have fallen into the same pharisaical spirit when fasting on a schedule. I certainly benefited from the bodily discipline of abstaining from food when appropriate, and I did draw near to God during those times, but also I was convicted by Holy Spirit of pride and religiosity. Though it has been thought of as a wonderful discipline to deny one's self, self-abasement can actually become self-focus as we turn us toward ourselves and our accomplishments instead of toward the person of Jesus Christ.

Contemporary Fasting

A food/ drink fast, though it is severe and difficult, may not be as effective in today's Western world as fasting from what captures our focus and our mind's attention. Abstaining from media, telecommunications, computer use and interaction with other people may in fact be much more effective in our goal of turning our full attention toward God. I suspect that, for many people, such a fast would be more of a challenge than going without meals.

Let us, for example, imagine that we stop eating and drinking, but continue to answer the phone, send text messages, read email, tweet our thoughts, or catch up on Facebook. Our food fast would certainly not bring the desired benefits, because we have not stilled and quieted our souls. The latter is what counts!

Retreating to Find Yourself in Him

Though I have enjoyed seasons of regular food fasting, I have more recently found that slowing down to spend days apart for personal retreat is what proves to be the most effective way to "fast".

In such a spirit of dedication, I commit to put aside all technology, media, and social activity to be alone with God; when it comes to seeking Him, that is for me the choice that appears most fruitful.

(I should mention that I do fast from food when Holy Spirit directs me. From my experience, this kind of fasting is more often for consecration to a new work or at the beginning of a new season in my life. Whether food is part of the fast is not as important as my motivation and dedication to being with God away from outside influences and distractions.)

A Call to Intimacy: Spiritual Retreat

I have come to view the call to fast as Holy Spirit's call to a special one-on-one time with God. In fact, I often feel the excitement one feels when asked to go on a special date with someone cherished! God is the lover of our souls and His desire for intimate times of communion is so much greater than we understand. The call to come away with God and spend some time in quietness and solitude is in a sense a fast from the "normal" life in favour of taking in more of God's fullness of life. I encourage you to welcome these times of fasting or slowing down to pay attention as God's invitation to draw near and give undivided focus to Him. Retreating into the presence of God can be done anywhere even right in your own home but I have found when you take time away from home, work, family it is best to be in a location where you are not constantly fighting the temptation to step back into everyday thoughts, time awareness, and habits.

I find a personal retreat becomes a like a pilgrimage of sorts. Once I have begun the time traveling to the place where I will spend my retreat God begins to show me things. The moment I step out of my door till I step in upon return is filled with meaning. It feels to me that God has been excitedly waiting for me to come away and draw near to Him. He orchestrates wonderful encounters with all kinds of signs and spiritual metaphors encrypted into messages of His heart to mine. I record in my journal everything that captures my attention on my journey and at the place of retreat so that none will be lost. It is such a pleasure to ponder each treasure and to marvel at the manifold ways He is communicating with me.

So I encourage you to take the times of retreat as Holydays with God to deepen your awareness and understanding of your friendship with God and His Kingdom within.

Suggested Meditation or Journaling Exercise

How would You, Lord, like to spend extended times with me?

Lord please speak to me about the practice of fasting.

Father what topic or scripture would you have me ponder or meditate.

Chapter 7 – Testing Revelation

Scripture makes it clear that it is essential to test the revelation we receive[49]. We must not disregard or make light of prophecy; it is God's voice to us directly or through another person! We need to discern that the message is indeed coming from the Spirit of God[50].

There are three possible sources of the spiritual messages we receive, no matter how they come to us. The sources are: The Spirit of Truth (God), human thinking or desires (human soul), or a lying spirit (demonic spirit). We begin our examination with that which is true and then discern the false, and finally we study our own desires.

The Spirit of Truth: God's Voice

Holy Spirit is the source of revelation; if we listen to His voice, He will show us how to apply it in our day-to-day lives. Therefore, it is imperative – a prerequisite, really - that we have invited Him to dwell within our spirits and that we are spending time with Him each day, talking and listening for what He has to say[51]. As He tells us in John 14:17, He will guide us into all truth. Living in this daily communion with God, we learn to discern His voice by the inner peace or

---

49   See 1 Corinthians 14:29 & 1 Thessalonians 5:21.
50   See 1 Corinthians 13:8-10.
51   See Deuteronomy 30:20 and Acts 5:32.

assurance of Holy Spirit, and can confidently receive guidance and encouragement from Him.

Before we begin to examine revelation, we must be sure we are prepared to receive Holy Spirit (the Spirit of Truth) by asking Him to cleanse us from all past shortcomings, mistakes, and unforgiveness of the faults of others. We need to renounce all other commitments and connections to any other god, anti-biblical world view or idol so that we can honestly confess that we have no other gods beside Father, Son, and Holy Spirit. Holy Spirit is the one who can speak to us from within, assure us of truth, and give discernment to know if what we are hearing is our own desires or a lying spirit, rather than Him.

God's Character and Nature

The more we know God, the easier it is to discern His voice. The names given to God are a big clue to His character and nature or ways. Following is a list of some of the names for the Father, Son, and Holy Spirit found in the Bible. See Appendix B for a full list of Scripture references.

God the Father: Almighty, Fortress, Healer, Heavenly Father, Holy One, I AM, Judge, King of Kings, The Lord is there, Lord of Lords, God is Love, Mighty God, Most High, My Banner, My Glory and the Lifter of my head, My Peace, My Righteousness.

God the Son: Lord Jesus Christ: Advocate, Almighty, Author and Finisher of Our Faith, Bread of Life, Captain of Salvation, Cornerstone, Creator, Day Spring, Deliverer, Desire of the Nations, The Door, Good Shepherd, Immanuel (God with us), King of Kings, Lamb of God, Life, Light of the World, The Vine, The Truth, The Way.

God the Holy Spirit: Comforter, Counsel, Fear of the Lord, Knowledge of God, Might, Our Guide, Peace, Spirit of Christ, Spirit of Holiness, Spirit of Truth & Wisdom & Understanding.

We test the revelation by comparing it with God's character and nature as encompassed by His names. In other words, if the revelation is in agreement with God's names, with His nature and character, we know it is from Him.

Nature: Holy, pure, good, perfect, just, righteous, loving, generous, gracious, merciful, forgiving, unifying, creative, abundant.

Fruit: Love, joy, peace, gentleness, goodness, faithfulness, meekness, moderation, trust, humility.

Lying or Deceitful Spirits: Enemy's Voices[52]

We can discern the negative voice of an enemy fairly easily because it aligns with his names, nature, and fruit. Listed below are some examples to assist you.

Names: The Enemy of God, The Devil, Satan, Deceiver, Father of Lies, Serpent, Accuser, Murderer, Thief, Robber, and a fallen angel of light.

Nature: prideful, boastful, arrogant, rude, selfish, unkind, greedy, and egotistical.

Fruit: (of Enemy revelation): sin, fear, disunity, depression, rage, low self-worth, pride, and loss of many kinds.

When the Deceiving Spirits hijack our thoughts and desires to make them work for the Enemy's purposes, they can become as an idol. Our longings and cravings are no longer in line with those God has designed for us; they get twisted, take our focus off of Him and onto ourselves, and indeed consume us as does dedication to a false god:

Our Inner Thoughts or God's Voice

Our cognitive, rational mind works to make decisions and think, or ponder, by our active choice. When we want to hear from God about a choice or decision in our lives, our own feelings and desires may interfere with hearing God. In order to distinguish our own inner voice from that of God's we first need to submit our will to God; we are to position ourselves to accept His answer regardless of whether it is what we desire in a particular situation. As we spend more time with God, we learn to distinguish between our own thoughts and

---

52   See Jeremiah 23:13.

preferences, and God's voice.

It is essential that we do not hold our own desires or opinions higher than God's will. We will not be able to hear or discern God's voice clearly if we are very passionate about receiving a certain answer: we will always hear what we want to hear if we have very strong feelings on a subject. In such a situation the answer we desire becomes too important and blocks God's answer.

In the example of the prophet Balaam, when he initially asked God about the offer of money to curse Israel, he received an answer which was certainly in line with God's character (God loves, blesses and favours His people). Because Balaam wanted in his heart to accept the money, he decided to check again, and this time heard the answer he wanted to hear; the money changed Balaam's ability to discern clearly because his desire for money was stronger than his desire for God's will.

We need to be able to receive any answer God gives so we must take the time to move from a strong desire to fulfill our will. By purposing to become neutral about decisions, we will accept God's divine choice; only then will we be positioned to hear clearly from God.

As we spend more time listening and talking with God, we learn His character. Knowing that His desire is to give us abundant life, that He will not with hold any good thing from us, helps to motivate us toward accepting His good perfect and pleasing will.

I have often had to wait to ask God about a decision or for His will on a topic till my desire was submitted to God's answer whatever it may be. It often takes time and prayer to be ready (in neutral mode) to hear what God wants and not to just hear what I want. The wait is always well worth it.

Aligning Revelation with Scripture

Scripture is our guide for confirmation; when we compare the revelation with Scripture, the Holy Spirit will reveal if it is compatible and in agreement with what God has already said. If what you have received (seen, heard, etc.) does not align with, or contradicts, what God has already said in the Bible, it is probably not God speaking.

There is an example of this in the Bible: Balaam the prophet[53] accepted money to curse Israel, despite God's previous command not to curse Israel. Because Balaam listened to the nation paying him to curse Israel, God intervened and set him straight through the words of a donkey.

This drastic example would not have been necessary if Balaam had used discernment to align the request of the enemy of Israel with God's nature (God is Love[54], The One Who blesses His people[55]) and what God had already spoken about blessing Israel. While Balaam did not have written scripture in his day, we do and can therefore use Scripture as a reference for what God has already said, and to learn about His character.

Testing Revelation by the Fruit or Results

At times, we can anticipate the outcome of an action or direction before we take it. We can, for example, tell whether it will lead to: loving God; loving our neighbour; bringing blessing, unity, or division among people; blessing and love, or away from love and blessing. At other times we will not fully realize the fruit or results till we have stepped out and the action actually comes to pass.

We need wisdom and sensitivity to Holy Spirit so we can discern the source of revelation, and then perceive (see and understand) what brings positive outcomes. Actions resulting from godly revelation will increase the fruit of the Spirit in our lives and the lives of those with whom we interact[56]. The outworking of Godly revelation is that we respond to those around us as Jesus would.

---

53   See Numbers 22:15-35.
54   See Deuteronomy 7:9; Psalm 36:7; Psalm 42:8; Joel 2:13; Jonah 4:2; Romans 8:39; 1 John 2:5, 3:1-10, and 4:6-8.
55   See Psalm 98:3 & Romans 12:14.
56   See Galatians 5:21-23 for a list of the fruit of the Spirit.

The Counsel of Others

Another safeguard when discerning God's voice is to share your revelation with some trusted friends. We find safety in the counsel of many, as the book of Proverbs instructs[57]. I have several close and trusted friends who hear God well and when I am in need of advice I know they will take time to go over what I feel God has revealed to me. I have done the same for others to bring reassurance and discernment. It is a blessing to find counsel with those who love God, are growing in their friendship with Him, and value listening to His voice.

Confirmation from God

Just as a loving father will carefully instruct and guide us, God in His great patience and kindness will make sure we understand His communication to us. As we learn to discern the voice of God, God confirms what He wants us to know. When we are not initially receiving or perhaps not understanding His message, He will show us in other ways.

For example, God may confirm an inner knowing that we need to give a financial gift through a dream, journaling of His voice, a Scripture or a prophetic word. Keep in mind that if we have no means to give it might not be a message from God. I had such an example.

I had such an experience at a prayer meeting many years ago, when I felt God was telling me to give my friend some money... yet I needed to do my family's groceries after the meeting. Toward the end of the meeting, the friend in question asked for prayer for a financial need - I thus had my confirmation. Although I had just enough money on me for our own family's needs, I nonetheless felt convicted to give my friend what the Lord told me to, which turned out to be the exact amount she needed!

I continued on to the grocery store with what money I had left and was greeted at the door by another friend; he gave me the exact amount I had just given away! Just a few moments earlier, he had felt compelled to repay money that I didn't even remember loaning him. God works in wonderful

---

57   See Proverbs 11:14, 15:22, 24:6.

ways to confirm the promptings of His voice!

Suggested Meditation or Journaling Exercise
Why is it important that I test the revelation I receive, Lord?

Does it align with God's character and nature?

Does this revelation align with Scripture?

What fruit or results will come from this?

Is this revelation from my inner thoughts or from God's voice?

Note the counsel of others who hear God.

Note the confirmations God has given.

Chapter 8 – Ministering Through the Spirit's Flow

Holy Spirit is the person of the Godhead Who is most intimate with us. As we have seen in previous chapters He carries all the attributes of God with the special mandate: to bring His character, gifts and fruit to the children of God and plant them into our nature. We have alluded to the fact that we are no longer merely human. As people of God we are sons and heirs with Christ. God has made us brothers of Jesus Christ, an extreme honour, which is hard to fathom, but true.

My friends we have this treasure in us which has been given from our loving Father for the purpose of bringing His kingdom of light to the world around us. As we live in union and agreement with God opportunities will be given to minister. Following are a few tools for ministry Holy Spirit has revealed to me which have enabled, and oiled my ministry. I trust you will ask Holy Spirit how these tools may help you.

Praying Like Jesus

Jesus sets us the example in how to pray. First and foremost Jesus was very personal with the Father. He enjoyed focused time with the Father every day when He went off by Himself to pray. Jesus lived in union with His Father, proclaiming in John 10:30,"I and the Father are one." Jesus also said, in John

5:19, that He was doing only what He saw His Father do.

In the Lord's Prayer from Matt 6:9 -18, Jesus gives us principles to guide us as we pray:

- Remember God is Father and He is holy so we need to love and revere Him.

- We need to be in agreement with God's kingdom to be instated on earth and His will is what we need to pray for.

- We can ask for our needs to be met.

- Forgiveness is essential to praying in agreement with God; if we don't forgive, we are out of alignment with His heart.

- Protection from evil is God's job: we can be secure in His protection.

- Fasting is a type of prayer. It is important to note that fasting needs to be done privately before God, otherwise it is ineffective - it can actually tempt us to be legalistic and religious.

Activation

To put into practice the model Jesus exemplified we need to use vision to look to see what He would like us to pray. We look to see what He is doing or saying before we pray, then pray according to His direction.

Here is an exercise to apply the principles covered in this section:

- Gather in small groups of 3 or 4 people and choose one person at a time to be the recipient of prayer.

- The prayer team gathers round the recipient and waits on the Holy Spirit to show them what Jesus is doing and saying then each one in turn prays according to Jesus' leading.

- If you feel comfortable, you may also share what you see Jesus do and hear Him say; note, however, that you may be giving a word of prophecy or of knowledge without actually praying for the recipient. Make sure you turn the revelation into a prayer so that the person receives the full benefit of what you have seen and heard the Lord direct you to pray.

• Proceed to pray for each individual in the group.

Suggested Meditation or Journaling Exercise
What do You want to say to me about praying like Jesus?

Releasing the Spirit's Flow

The wonder of life in connection with God goes far beyond our human understanding. Being indwelt by the Holy Spirit is, in itself, supernatural (beyond - or greater than – "natural"). We have discussed the attributes of Holy Spirit, the gifts and fruit He brings as we live from His presence, but the ability to choose to release His flow, is truly an amazing privilege. Choosing to release the flow of Holy Spirit Brings godly change to our own behaviour and positively effects the world around us

What I am about to share has radically changed my life and the lives of everyone who chooses to live this way. We being God's children, His sons, and co-heirs with Christ are able to release the power of the indwelling Holy One by choice.

Dr. Mark Virkler and his wife Patty have an excellent book and DVD teaching which details the scriptural foundation and methodology of this practice[58]. I thank them wholeheartedly for this gift to us all. Below is my own understanding and experience on the spiritual practice of releasing the kingdom from within and, in so doing, living from the flow of God's Spirit.

_____

58   Dr. Virkler's book and teaching, available from cwgministries.org, are called "Naturally Supernatural".

Death to the Flesh

> *I have been crucified with Christ: it is no longer I who lives, but Christ lives in me; and the life which I now live in the flesh I live by faith in the Son of God, Who loved me and gave Himself for me. (Galatians 2:20)*

The Scriptures recommend that we reckon ourselves dead to our human resources (flesh) so that we may live from God's resources[59]. If we live according to our abilities and understanding we will remain within our own nature which, according to the Scripture, is death. However, if we live from the unction and flow of the Holy Spirit we will see life and peace result.

The Divine Exchange

The Spirit who raised Christ from the dead lives in us and is ready to quicken our mortal bodies for the purpose of victory and empowerment because we are the sons of God[60]. In fact when we are filled with the Holy Spirit we are indeed putting on Christ with all of His attributes[61]. Jesus Christ is alive in us by His Spirit and we have become His body here on earth we because we house Holy Spirit. As we grow in our awareness of the fact, that the Spirit of God indwells us, we begin to yield to His life instead of living from our own abilities.

Alive to the Spirit

Though I had memorized Galatians 2:20 in my early years as a Christian, I did not realize it was possible to actually live accordingly.

As I matured in my relationship with God, I discovered that we live out this Scripture by agreement with it and

---

59   See Romans 8:5-6.
60   See Romans 8:11-14.
61   See Galatians 3:26-27.

yielding our human faculties, abilities, and resources to the flow of Holy Spirit within us. For example; instead trying to love an individual with our human love, we draw on the love of God which resides within us due to Holy Spirits indwelling.

The Prayer of Release and the Inward Flow

In very practical terms I do not live by my resources to fix a situation or by trying harder not to sin for example. I simply admit to God my inability and then release His power from within to take over.

Following is a sample releasing prayer for the purposes of overcoming temptation:

"Lord Jesus, You are the sinless one. The power to overcome sin is in You. Thank You that You live in me. I now release Your power to overcome this temptation."

When releasing the flow of Holy Spirit we focus on the spirit within us which is our spirit in union with Holy Spirit. By the act of our will, choosing to yield to the Spirit, we release the flow of the Holy Spirit. As we command our spirit through the prayer of release, it firstly bubbles up in union with Holy Spirit to flow through my soul (mind, will, and emotions). Then, since Spirit is not limited to the confines of my body, it continues out to push back my enemy, the temptation, and effectively changes the spiritual atmosphere around me. We can choose to release God's power from within us in this way adapting the above prayer according to the situation.

Releasing to Others

It is Important to check our motive in releasing the spirit with in us to others. If we have a tainted motive: that of manipulating or controlling a situation for our own benefit we are in danger of entering into agreement with the enemy of God and a spirit of witchcraft. If I am to serve my fellow man by the use of releasing the Holy flow of spirit, I need to stay correctly focused on the fruit of God's Spirit and release:

love, joy, peace patience, kindness, goodness, faithfulness, gentleness, and temperance. As the scriptures say there is no law against these things so we are completely safe releasing them. Also we may be led to release the flow of holiness or purity depending on what we sense is needed.

When I need love and grace for someone, instead of trying to muster them up from my limited store, I turn to Holy Spirit's unlimited resources and activate the release by praying a prayer such as: "Holy Spirit, I cannot love this person. My grace is not enough so I choose to release Your love and Your grace to them now in Jesus' name."

I then focus on the Spirit once again, actively agreeing with God's love and grace to arise in me. The Spirit's flow causes love and grace to bubble up through me first, then to move out into the atmosphere, permeating it, flowing to the person who is the recipient.

Often a noticeable change occurs, in me as well as the other person. Note, for instance, as you practice this discipline that you will begin to sense God's emotions washing you, filling you, with love toward the individual. This not only changes your attitude toward them but the person also begins to feel the comfort and love of God which in turn changes them.

Releasing the Kingdom of Heaven into the Atmosphere

We can release God's peace into the atmosphere of a place where we may be sensing contention or strife. Those who are struggling will be calmed by the release of the Spirit and the enemy is silenced by His power. Our command does not have to be spoken audibly as the Spirit is well able to hear our thoughts. God communes with our spirit so He knows what we are thinking and our desires even before we have formed thoughts into language.

As we progress in this practice, carrying the power of God, this treasure, in earthen vessels[62], we find we begin to

---

62   See 2 Corinthians 4:7.

naturally release without hesitation. This automatic release is what I call "leaking" Holy Spirit. Living in communion with God, we are filled to overflowing so the wonderful unction of God (sometimes called "the anointing") will spill out, gently changing things around us for good wherever we go.

Being Proactive for the Kingdom

Actively releasing the flow of Holy Spirit enables us to live according to Jesus' proclamation in John 7:37-39 that rivers of living water shall flow from within us. As I have mentioned, there are times when without knowing we are leaking the flow of Holy Spirit; more often, however, we need to choose and discipline ourselves to agree with God that our human effort must step aside and allow the Spirit of God to do the work. We cannot do what God can: Scripture tells us that without Him we can do nothing (of spiritual impact). Yet with Him and by His power we can do all things[63].

As you live through the flow of the Holy Spirit you will find wonderful opportunities arise to help others by releasing the flow of God and watching Him work. I have often released God's peace in the grocery store when I could see the anger and frustration among family members, patience having worn thin. What a joy it has been to witness the results: a frustrated mother softening, a rambunctious child calming down, or a previously tense husband and wife beginning to smile at each other, as they experience the peace and love of God envelop them. The peace of God is so powerful that it guards hearts, minds, and prevents tears too.

Actions Inspired by the Flow

There is another aspect or benefit to releasing the flow of Holy Spirit. The spontaneous thoughts or ideas that may accompany releasing the Spirit are His additional help for the situation you are facing. These thoughts and ideas are the prompting of Holy Spirit to do or say something in addition to

---

63   John 15:5 and Philippians 4:13

the silent activation you have engaged in.

We often do not need to speak as we minister the release; we may simply be in need of information that God is sharing and so do not need to speak them out. On the other hand, sometimes Holy Spirit-prompting is given for wise or calming words; God downloads the perfect response to us so we are well advised to speak out what He is saying! He will give us the sense of weather to speak or not in each situation...hence the need to learn to hear and discern His voice.

The power of God will change us, the atmosphere, and people around us. The question is: will we discipline ourselves to turn to that power? God is willing, His power is always available, so let us not be slow to learn to live through it that we may infuse the world with the atmosphere of heaven.

Hindrances to Releasing God's Flow

God is able to show His strength even in our weakness He can show Himself strong. We can be sure God will do wonderful things in and through us, but how much better to be in agreement with Him completely and to be free to release the power of Holy Spirit through our spirit to actively affect the world around us for good in agreement with His nature.

There are several things that can hinder the release of the Spirit's power through us.

- Unconfessed Sin can cause us to be dull of spirit so that we miss the promptings of the Spirit of God or that we feel disconnected and guilt laden. The answer to sin is to confess and repent. The blood of Jesus has paid for all sin, so there is no need to be hindered for a second, let Jesus deal with sin as quickly as possible and be free.

- Being offended by people and situation can be a barrier to ministering from the flow of Holy Spirit. Not letting go of an offence is unforgiveness which is a definite hindrance to hearing God's voice and ministering His love. We need to give Jesus every hurt and offence and let go of the pain. Then we are set free to love and bless without blockage.

- Forgetting who we are in God often causes us to lean on our own resources and try to fix people or situations. We need to remember we are vessels of the Most High God and as such we contain the river of God which can flow from within us and bring God's solutions. Though we may have human wisdom and resources they do not compare to what God's power will do. We must let go of trying to do things in our strength and step back into our sonship.

- Focusing upon the problem at hand instead of focusing on Jesus will give us a wrong perspective. We could be pulled into wants and needs instead of God's will for the situation. We need to focus on Jesus, tune into what Holy Spirit is saying, and then release the flow according to God's prompting.

Activation

We may practice this discipline with a friend who would also like to grow in this area.

- Stand facing each other but do not touch.

- One person then actively, but silently, commands God's love to be released to the other who focuses on receiving. It is helpful if you picture the flow being released as is spoken of in Scripture, rivers of living water flowing from your belly. (The front cover of this booklet illustrates it quite well.) Allow a minute or two for the receiver to sense with their spirit, emotions, and body.

- The receiver gives testimony to what they felt. Then switch so that the flow is released through the individual who started by receiving.

- Next, try releasing one of the other fruit of the Spirit to each other: spend time experiencing and sharing what you feel.

- You may like to experiment by not telling each other which of the fruit of the Spirit you are releasing and have the receiver discern what is flowing to them.

This exercise demonstrates the truth of the releasing principle, as well as developing discernment in with all of our faculties.

Suggested Meditation or Journaling Exercise

Lord, what do You want to say to me about the importance of living from Your holy flow?

Lord, speak to me about releasing Your flow into a situation where I am currently struggling.

Chapter 9 – Team Work

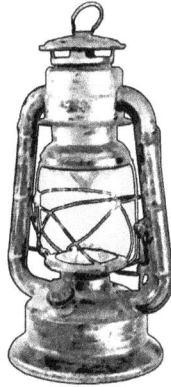

1 Corinthians 12:7-20 speaks of the Body of Christ being diverse but all part of the same body, each one equally important. Therefore, we need to honour one another and value what every person has to give. We are to make room for one another wherever we meet.

Whether it is to worship or minister in prayer, "every joint supplies", meaning: Each person holds a piece of the puzzle God wants to put together for the good of His Kingdom and His dear children. Each of us has different gifts of the Spirit, tools which are especially given by God to be used under the direction of Holy Spirit, the architect or designer of the Kingdom of God. We each have our own unique part to play and place to work.

Prophetic Etiquette

How can we accomplish this love and respect between us, practically speaking? We can only do what our Father shows, that for which He empowers us. By His grace, we will love and honour each other; indeed, when we honour each other He is very pleased. One way we can position ourselves for this good work is to come together in Holy Spirit-led teams. Holy Spirit is resident in every born-again believer so we need to allow Him to have a voice and act through each person on the team.

Some may be more confident or more experienced,

however this does not necessarily mean they are the leaders or that they should do most of the ministry. There are occasions when it is best that they hold back so as to bring confirmation, encouragement, and opportunity to the newer or less experienced individuals on the team. If we are in ministry for the glory of the King and the furtherance of His Kingdom, we will desire to see others learn and progress, which can mean we take a servant position, saying and doing less on a team.

Sometimes, mentoring and teaching are called for so that others can receive fresh revelation: the teacher must teach and the mentor must activate his or her comrade. In short, the work of the body is accomplished best if every member participates. Wise teachers or mentors allow mistakes and imperfect even messy sessions of activation so every member can learn and grow to maturity.

Holy Spirit is very good at teaching and leading; if we yield to Him and let go of our desire to control, He will do so much better than a human leader could! While it is easy to recognize the team model described in principle, it is not so easy to deny our ambitions, self-actualization, need to control, and fears of what could happen, all of which may surface when we take on a less active role.

When Personal Excitement Interrupts Group Experience

At times we may have very tangible encounters with God that can be exciting and even overwhelming; these wonderful experiences may bring us to states where we are beside ourselves as we give way to Holy Spirit at work in us. Such connections with God can be beneficial in bringing direction, clarity, or fresh insights to a group (for example in prayer or ministry times).

However, we are to handle such experiences with care, as physical manifestations in one or a few individuals can disrupt a meeting. In fact, one person's encounter can actually interrupt what Holy Spirit is already doing in the group as a whole.

I have experienced and noted in others on occasion

physical manifestations such as overwhelming laughter or shaking whilst in a group prayer session. On the occasions that this happens, it may be best if the overwhelmed individual goes into another room or moves away from the ministry team so that their experience does not detract from other people's focus on God.

There are other occasions when revelation comes to us that our enthusiasm to tell others can hinder the flow of the Spirit following is an example:

Following a time of prayer at a conference in Pennsylvania, Rachelle had a personal encounter with Jesus where He communicated with her in a very physical, real way. In her enthusiasm, she rushed to the front and was tempted to grab a mike so she could share with the large crowd the words and visions she had received, to encourage and edify the body of believers gathered there.

She opted instead to speak with leader Lou Engle to hear from him how to proceed. His response startled her: Lou believed what she had experienced was a wonderful encounter with Christ... for her. He gently and wisely pointed out that her revelation was a personal one, and that it was not necessarily for the crowd as a whole at that time.

The leader did not minimize the wonder and awe of what Rachelle had seen and heard, yet he discerned that her revelation was individual rather than for group application. We too need to be mindful of and sensitive to the interests both of the group and of the individuals that make it up.

We need to give grace to our fellow team members as they too may be overcome with excitement and a sense of urgency when they meet God in an intense way. Another person may be prompted by Holy Spirit to take the team member away from where the group is gathered; this gives the opportunity to minister to the team member, providing freedom, support and encouragement, or a listening ear as the need may be, while allowing the group to move forward with their focused time. This is also needed if the person is having personal negative issues, once again the group can continue with their focus while we take the struggling person aside and minister privately to their need.

In summary, given that a personal encounter with God can be overwhelming, we need to be respectful of the environment we are in at the time. If we find ourselves in the context of a group, let's be sensitive to the focus on God and His work as well as our fellow team members.

Seeking God Together for Wisdom and Direction

Working together in agreement with Holy Spirit is God's design for Christian ministry. The team of believers can be as small as two (couples and ministry partnerships) or as large as the leadership team or prayer cell. No matter how large or small the group unity of agreement is very powerful and essential in modeling the strategy God has for His body, the Church.

When believers need to make decisions that affect their joint ministry it is very helpful for the group to have a dedicated amount of time in which they may individually seek God for guidance. I have found soaking or listening prayer along with journaling God's voice very helpful disciplines for this application.

After the designated time has elapsed (the soaking and journaling session or perhaps some days of seeking God) the group can come together to share what each one feels God has expressed to them. Many times there is a common thread of agreement and wisdom which encourages the group to either move ahead or not to choose the proposition at that time.

However, there are times when seeking the Lord as a group or couple that agreement does not follow. If this is the case the group needs to wait and keep seeking God's guidance.

Some Reasons For Differences in Discerning What God is Saying

- One or more in the group is mistaken in what they are hearing God say; perhaps they are being swayed by strong opinions or feelings.

- The timing is not quite right to go ahead so the group must wait till God aligns everyone, at which time things will properly fall into place.

- Perhaps the members are not of one mind as to the purpose of seeking God. In this case each person may need to voice to the group what they perceive the focus is for the time of seeking God. The question we are asking God must be the same and be understood by each member.

- There is the possibility that the proposed change or idea we have is not God's choice. In that case we need to step away from the plan and wait on God for His better one.

What to do when you do not agree:

When the body of believers is faced with feelings of division, they need to go to the unifying One, the Spirit of Jesus Christ, because He is our common denominator. Holy Spirit is the Spirit of love and unity; He is able to bring agreement with each other and Himself. We need to take time apart (time-out) to hear from Him and give Him time to work in each person. If the group will wait, and listen, they will learn God's heart for each situation and receive wisdom for interpersonal relationships.

In this active kind of "waiting" or taking a step back from the first impulse to intervene and humanly make things work, each person in the group submits to the leading of Holy Spirit: thus allowing time for agreement to be reached. The unity that agreement brings is also a confirmation of God's direction and timing. If we force agreement or submit to pressure we will not truly be hearing from God. Where there is no agreement in Spirit we cannot move into supernatural work.

When We Sense Disunity in a Group Prayer Time

My experience has been that the simplest and best solution for working through any sense of disunity is to pray in our prayer language (see "Evidences of Holy Spirit Infilling", Chapter 4). We know Holy Spirit will always bring us into agreement with the purposes of God's kingdom. If we allow Him to pray through us by use of our prayer language our prayers will be perfect and our hearts will be in tune with Him also. Again we need to be patient and wait on God for His wisdom to flow.

Releasing the Spirit supernaturally from within, as described in chapter 7, is very helpful. Whether in a large group prayer time or one-on-one, we can be vehicles for God's love, peace, and agreement. It can be hard, when everything within us wants to act in our own interest or what we feel is God's interest. Emotions can be very powerful so choosing to defer to God and prefer others over ourselves is an act of submission which, if we ask, will be empowered by the Holy Spirit. The more we practice releasing the flow of God's grace under pressure the more it will become our first response and our human reactions will take a back seat. When emotions are high we need Holy Spirit to settle them so that we do not overstate our case or become overly emphatic.

The Foundation of Love

If a foundation of love and relationship is well rooted, we can communicate our feelings honestly and respectfully. Even in the best of human connections, however, we need to be sure that our emotions are at peace and that there is little possibility of accusation or fault-finding, before we proceed to address something difficult with the others involved. Once again releasing the peace and love of God will calm us and those around us before we address difficult subjects.

It is worth all we give or relinquish to be an active, functioning part of our Lord's Body, the Church. As iron sharpens iron, so we are challenged through relationships with others, and brought to maturity and good character by His love. While we are being continually transformed Holy Spirit softens us to be changed, conforming us to the image of Jesus, so that we become the pure and spotless bride. This bride metaphor that scripture uses is true for us individually, as well as the body of believers (collective Bride of Christ). As we live together in unity the world at large will notice the supernatural edge in our willingness to come together in love and agreement.

Suggested Meditation or Journaling Exercise

Holy Spirit, what do You want to say to me about my place in Your body?

Appendix A: Bible References – Dreams

OLD TESTAMENT

Gen. 31:24 Jacob

Gen. 37:5-20 Joseph

Gen. 40:5-16 Prisoners

Gen. 41:1 Pharaoh

Num. 12:6 God Communicates

Judg. 7:13 Jericho Guard

1 Kings 3:5 Solomon

Dan. 1:17 King Nebu - Statue

Dan. 4:5 King Nebu - Tree Dream

Hab. 2:3 Man Among Myrtles

NEW TESTAMENT

Matt. 1:20 Joseph

Matt. 2:12 Wise Men

Matt. 2:13 Joseph

Matt. 2:19 Joseph

Matt. 2:22 Joseph

Matt. 27:19 Pilate's Wife

Acts 2:17 Sons & Daughters

Acts 16:9 Man from Macedonia

Appendix B: Bible References – Visions

OLD TESTAMENT

Gen. 15:1 Abraham

Num. 22:31 Balaam

Num. 24:2 Balaam

1 Sam. 28:6 of Samuel by Medium

2 Sam. 24:11 of Gad to David

1 Chron. 29:29 "Seer Prophets"

2 Chron. 19:2 Hanani the Seer

Ps. 89:19 God Speaks by Dream and Vision

Ps. 123:1 Psalmist

Isa. 6:1 Isaiah's Call

Isa. 17 Destruction of Damascus

Isa. 21:2 Babylon Plundered

Isa. 22:1 Jerusalem in Uproar

Isa. 28:7 Priests & Prophets

Ezek. 1:14 Ezekiel at Kedar River.

Ezek. 8:3 To Jerusalem By Hair

Ezek. 10:1 Lord's Glory Leaving

Ezek. 40:2 Heavenly Temple

Ezek. 43:1 Glory Filling Temple

Dan. 5:5 Writing Finger

Dan. 7:1 Daniel's Four Beasts

Amos: Seer, Book of Visions

Joel: Prophecies Are Visionary.

Obadiah: Seer, Book of Visions

Micah: Seer, Book of Visions

Nahum: 1:1 about Nineveh

Habakkuk: Seer, Book of Visions

Zechariah: Seer, Book of Visions

NEW TESTAMENT

Matt. 13:16 Dove/ Holy Spirit

Mark 9:8 Cloud of the Presence.

Luke 1:22 Zachariah in the Temple

Luke 24:31 Road to Emmaus

Acts 2:17 Sons and Daughters will...

Acts 7:55 Stephen's Vision.

Acts 9:10 Ananias about Paul

Acts 10:3 Cornelius' of Angel

Acts 10:17 Peter (Sheet)

Acts 18:9 Paul's Vision of God

Acts 26:18 Paul's Vision of Jesus

Revelation: A Book of Visions of the Apostle John

Appendix C: Bible References – Names of God

The following list of the names of God is given in the order that each name is revealed in Scripture. The name is given, then in brackets the pronunciation, after which come the Scripture reference and finally the meaning of each name.

GOD THE FATHER: Hebrew Meanings

Elohim: (el-lo-Heem) Gen. 1:1 God who has authority, sovereignty, creative power

Yahweh: (yah- WEH) Gen. 2:4 also known as Jehovah, Lord, salvation for God's from slavery

El-Elyon: (EL el-YOHN) Gen. 14:17-20 most high God, exalted one, highest

El-Roi: (EL raw-EE) Gen. 16:11 God who sees me, the strong one

El-Shaddai: (EL shad-DAI) Gen. 17:1 Mighty God, God of the mountains, God Almighty

Yahweh-Yireh: (yah-WEH jir-EH) Gen .22:13-14 the Lord will provide

Yahweh-Rophe: (yah-WEH row-FEH) Exod. 16:28 the Lord who heals

Yahweh-Nissi: (yah-WEH nis-SEE) Exod. 17:15 the Lord our banner

Yahweh-Maccaddeshem: (yah-WEH mak-ka-DESH-shem) Exod. 31:13 the Lord my sanctifier, the Lord who makes us holy

Yahweh Shalom: (yah-WEH sha-LOME) Judg. 6:24 the Lord is peace

Yahweh Roi: (yah-WEH row-EE) Ps. 23:1 the Lord is my shepherd

Yahweh Tsebaoth: (yah-WEH tes-ba-OATH) Isa. 6:1-3 the

Lord of Hosts

El-Olam: (EL o-LAM) Isa. 40:28-31 the everlasting God, eternal one

Yahweh-Tsidqenu: (yah- WEH tsid-KAY-nu) Jer. 23:6 the Lord our righteousness

Yahweh-Shammah: (yah-WEH SHA-mah) Ezek. 48:35 the Lord who is present, the Lord is there

Adonay: (a-do-NAI) Mal. 1:6 Lord, master, the lordship of God

GOD THE SON: Names and Symbols

The last Adam: 1 Cor. 15:20

Advocate: 1 John 1:1

Almighty: Rev. 1:8

Alpha: Rev. 1:8 & 21:6

Amen: Rev. 3:14

Angel of the Lord: Gen. 16:9-14

Anointed: Ps. 2:2

Apostle: Heb. 3:1

Author: Heb. 12:2

Baby born of Mary: Luke 2:16

Branch: Zech. 3:8

Bread of life: John 6:35

Bridegroom: Matt. 9:15

Bright and morning star: Rev. 22:16

Carpenter: Matt. 13:55

Chief Shepherd: 1 Pet. 5:4

Christ: Matt. 1:16, 2:4

Commander: Isa. 55:4

Consolation of Israel: Luke 2:25

Cornerstone: Eph. 2:20

Dayspring: Luke 1:78

Day Star: 2 Pet. 1:19

Dearly Loved Son: Eph. 1:6

Deliver: Rom. 11:26

Desire of the Nations: Hag. 2:7

Door: John 10:9

Emmanuel: Matt. 1:23

Everlasting Father: Isa. 9:6

Express Image of God: Heb. 1:3

Faithful Witness: Rev. 1:5, 3:14

First Fruit: 1 Cor. 15:23

Forerunner: Heb. 6:20

Foundation: Isa. 28:16

Fountain: Zech. 13:1

Friend of sinners: Matt. 11:19

Gift of God: 2 Cor. 9:15

Gate of the sheepfold: John 10:7

Glory of God: Isa. 60:1

God: John 1:1, Rom. 9:5, 1 Tim. 3:16

Good Shepherd: John 10:11,14

Governor: Matt. 2:6

Great Shepherd: Heb. 13:20

Guardian of our souls: 1 Pet. 2:25

Guide: Ps. 48:14

Head of the Church: Col. 1:18

High Priest: Heb. 3:1, 7:1

Holy One of God: Mark 1:24

Holy One of Israel: Isa. 41:14

Judge: Mic. 5:1, Acts 10:42

King of Israel: Matt. 27:42

Lamb of God: John 1:29, 36

Lawgiver: Isa. 33:22

Life: John 14:6

Light of the World: John 1:41, 9:5

Lion of the tribe of Judah: Rev. 5:5

Lord of Lords: Rev. 19:16

Master: Matt. 8:19

Mediator: 1 Tim. 2:5

Messiah: Dan. 9:25

Mighty God: Isa. 9:6

Nazarene: Mark 1:24

Only Begotten Son: John 1:18

Physician: Matt. 9:12

Power of God: 1 Cor. 1:24

Prince: Acts 5:31

Propitiation: 1 John 2:2

Purifier: Mal. 3:3

Priest: Heb. 4:14

Rabbi: John 3:2

Ransom: 1 Tim. 2:6

Redeemer: Isa. 59:20

Refiner: Mal. 3:3

Refuge: Isa. 25:4

Resurrection: John 11:25

Righteousness: Jer. 23:6

Rock: Deut 32:15

Rod, Shoot, Branch: Isa. 11:1

Root of David: Rev. 22:16

Sacrifice: Eph. 5:2

Saviour: Luke 1:47, 2:11

Seed of Abraham & David: Gal. 3:16, 2 Tim. 2:8

Seed of a woman: Gen. 3:15

Servant: Isa. 49:7

Shiloh: Gen. 49:10

Son of David: Matt. 15:22

Son of God: Luke 1:35

Son of Man: Matt. 18:11

Son of Mary: Mark 6:3

Son of the Most High: Luke 1:32

Source of God's Creation: Rev. 3:14

Stone: Matt. 21:42, Acts 4:11

Sun of Righteousness: Mal. 4:2

Teacher: Matt. 26:18

Truth: John 14:6

True Vine: John 15:1

Way: John 14:6

Wisdom of God: 1 Cor. 1:24

Wonderful: Isa. 9:6

Word: Rev. 19:13

HOLY SPIRIT: Specific Names & Symbols

As the Spirit of Jesus Christ the Holy Spirit carries all of the attributes of Jesus, many of the Names of Christ apply to Holy Spirit as well as those listed below.

Counsellor: John 14:26

Comforter: John 14:26

Eternal Spirit: Heb. 9:14

Seven Fold Spirit: Isa. 11:1-2

Spirit of Adoption: Rom. 8:15

Spirit of Christ: Rom. 8:9

Spirit of Glory: 1 Pet. 4:14

Spirit of God: 1 Cor. 3:16

Spirit of Grace: Heb. 10:29

Spirit of Holiness: Rom. 1:4

Spirit of Life: Rom. 8:2

Spirit of Promise: Acts 1:4-5

Spirit of Resurrection: Rom. 1:4

Spirit of Revelation: Eph. 1:17

Spirit of truth: John 16:13

Spirit of Wisdom: Isa. 11:2, Eph. 1:17

Thank You

It is my prayer that you have found this book helpful in your friendship with God. I would love to hear from you and it would be most helpful to have feedback. I encourage you to write a review to help other readers decide on this book.

Other Books

Divine Focus
Living in Union with God
Arranged as a trilogy, Divine Focus explores the subject of practicing the presence of Christ. It explains how humans may live in complete agreement with Father, Son and Holy Spirit. Communion with God moment by moment is modeled beautifully by our Jesus Christ, so each of the sections of this trilogy are named after His self-description.

Section 1: **"The Life"** examines Jesus Christ as our example and teacher on the subject of living in perfect focus.

Section 2: **"The Truth"** contains essays on truths which explain the path and process of being tuned to the presence of God.

Section 3: **"The Way"** details disciplines and practices which Christians through the ages have used to connect in intimate friendship with God.

Listen Up!
Discerning the voice of God for your everyday life.
Jesus said, "My sheep know My voice" – and you can tune in and hear from God every day. You will find in this little book practical and easy-to-understand keys for unlocking the door to knowing God's voice. As you read and work through the listening prayer exercises, you will find the pleasure of knowing the One who made you. God has a beautiful plan for your life and you can discover His voice, take His lead, and follow the path Jesus has marked out for you.

Chapters include:
- Hearing With More Than Ears: The Ways God Speaks
- The Faith Factor: The Key That Unlocks Supernatural Life

- Stop Look & Listen: Journaling Your Conversations With God
- Discerning Direction: Knowing What the Signs Say
- Christian Meditation: Using The Grey Matter and More
- Checking It Out: God? Satan? Or Just Wishful Thinking?
- How Others Have Learned to Listen Up

The Restoration Work Book for Participants

A Guide to Restoring the Soul Through Inner-Healing
Developed from Biblical techniques, this approach to prayer counselling is used for Inner Healing of the personality or soul. It is a practical tool to enable every Christian to pray through areas of blockage and emotional pain. Once learned, this method can be used in subsequent areas of emotional pain and blockages to continue on the road of healing and restoration using the reproducible work sheets provided.

Chapter Headings:
- The Wounded Soul
- Seven Steps for Restoring the Soul
- Restoring Generational Lines
- Correcting Soul Ties
- Healing Painful Memories
- Renouncing Negative Words
- Renewing Truth and Purpose
- Cleansing from the Demonic
- Living by Holy Spirit's Power
- Aftercare
- Reproducible Resources

The Restoration Work Book Leaders Guide

A Leaders Guide to Restoring the Soul Through Inner-Healing
The Leader's Edition of the workbook is a manual for leaders
of the restoration workshops. This book includes all material
in Participant Guide as well as additional helps and methods to
assist Inner-Healing leaders. This guide also contains prayers
of repentance from Freemasonry.

The Language of Dreams and Visions

A Handbook for Interpretation and Symbolism
This handbook is a guide to understanding and interpreting
dreams and visions. It contains an extensive and valuable
dictionary of biblical and cultural symbols giving insight into
God's way of communication. It includes a template dream
journal for recording and interpreting dreams.

Chapters include:
- God Is Speaking
- Supernatural Encounters
- Defining Dream and Vision
- Restoring Dream and Visionary Capacities
- Soaking or Listening Prayer
- Dream and Vision Recording
- Interpretation
- Testing Revelation
- Dictionary of Symbols
- Biblical Reference Section for Dreams, Visions and
  Bible References for the Names of God

Destiny Purpose and Calling

*Understanding and Fulfilling Your Unique Place in God's
Kingdom on Earth*
A straight-forward, practical guide to bring you along in your
journey of discovery as to who God has designed you to be,
where you are in your journey of purpose in Him and what you

next step along His path is. Every chapter includes action steps to intentionally move you into your purpose and calling so you may enjoy the journey into Kingdom destiny.

Chapters include:
- The Books of Destiny – My Legacy
- Created for Purpose
- Kingdom Calling
- Check the Baggage
- Personal Identity – Where Have I Come From? Who am I? Why am I Here?
- Gifts From God – Discerning My Spiritual Gifts
- Talents & Skills – Discerning My Abilities
- Additions or Distractions
- Tracking With God – Where am I @?
- Finding My Life in Him – Where am I Going?
- Getting to My Destination

About Yvonne

Once a native of Australia, Yvonne lives and works in Canada. She has been married to her husband Bob for more than 45 years. They have five grown children and eight adorable grandchildren. Yvonne has been a friend of God for over 40 years and is growing to love Him more each year. Under God's direction and anointing Yvonne produces:

- Customized prayer blankets
- Scripture meditation CD's
- Manuals & books on topics such as inner-healing, listening prayer, meditation, interpreting dreams and visions, knowing the Holy Spirit, and discerning destiny

Rev. Yvonne Prentice,

Pastor at His Presence Ministries

Credentialed with ECCiC

Yvonne brings encouragement and hope to many. She loves to introduce others to the practice of "soaking" or listening prayer, and Biblical meditation. She loves to foster times in God's presence helping others deepen their friendship with Jesus Christ. Regularly ministering at retreats and workshops, Yvonne's heart is to see God's people grow in intimacy with Jesus Christ by practicing His presence daily.

Contact

Email: hispresenceministries@gmail.com

Facebook: through her page *His Presence Ministries.*

Blog: pushingtheedges.blogspot.com

www.ingramcontent.com/pod-product-compliance
Lightning Source LLC
Chambersburg PA
CBHW072003060426
42446CB00042B/1786